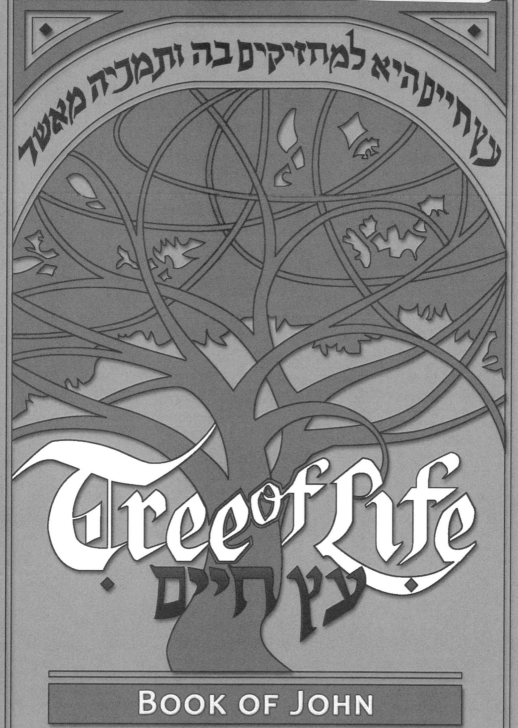

W9-ASY-131

עץ חיים היא למחזיקים בה ותמכיה מאשר

Tree of Life
עץ חיים

BOOK OF JOHN

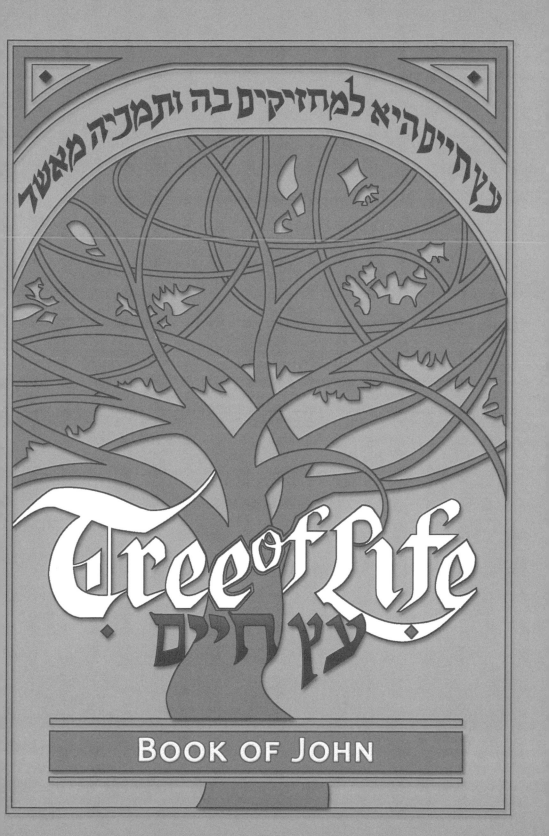

עֵץ חַיִּים הִיא לַמַּחֲזִיקִים בָּהּ וְתֹמְכֶיהָ מְאֻשָּׁר

Tree of Life
עֵץ חַיִּים

BOOK OF JOHN

© Copyright 2010–The Messianic Jewish Family Bible Project

All rights reserved. This book is protected by the copyright laws of the United States of America. This book may not be copied or reprinted for commercial gain or profit. The use of short quotations or occasional page copying for personal or group study is permitted and encouraged. Permission will be granted upon request. Unless otherwise identified, Scripture quotations are from the Tree of Life Version (TLV). Copyright 2010 by Destiny Image. Please note that Destiny Image's publishing style capitalizes certain pronouns in Scripture that refer to the Father, Son, and Holy Spirit, and may differ from some publishers' styles. Take note that the name satan and related names are not capitalized. We choose not to acknowledge him, even to the point of violating grammatical rules.

DESTINY IMAGE® PUBLISHERS, INC.

P.O. Box 310, Shippensburg, PA 17257-0310

"Speaking to the Purposes of God for This Generation and for the Generations to Come."

This book and all other Destiny Image, Revival Press, MercyPlace, Fresh Bread, Destiny Image Fiction, and Treasure House books are available at Christian bookstores and distributors worldwide.

For a U.S. bookstore nearest you, call 1-800-722-6774.

For more information on foreign distributors, call 717-532-3040.

Reach us on the Internet: www.destinyimage.com.

ISBN 13 TP: 978-0-7684-3613-6

ISBN 13 HC: 978-0-7684-3614-3

ISBN 13 LP: 978-0-7684-3615-0

ISBN 13 Ebook: 978-0-7684-9049-7

For Worldwide Distribution, Printed in the U.S.A.

1 2 3 4 5 6 7 8 9 10 11 / 13 12 11 10

Messianic Jewish Family Bible Project

Board of Directors

Rabbi Mark Greenberg
Messianic Jewish Family Bible Project, Chairman of the Board

Rabbi Kirk Gliebe
Union of Messianic Jewish Congregations, Vice President

Margaret Kowalski MD
Messianic Jewish Family Bible Project, Treasurer

Susan Perlman
Jews for Jesus, Vice President

Arnis Sprancmanis, Esq.
Messianic Jewish Family Bible Project, Secretary

Rabbi Steve Weiler
International Alliance of Messianic Congregations and Synagogues, Executive Officer

Sarah Weiner
Jewish Voice Ministries International, Director of Communications

Biblical Text Development Team

Biblical Text Management Team

Rabbi Jeffrey E. Feinberg, M.Div., Ph.D.
Patricia K. Feinberg, M.S.T., M.A.
Etz Chaim Messianic Congregation, UMJC

Original Text Production

Rabbi Stephen Galiley, M.Div.
Deborah Galiley B.A.
Beit Shalom Messianic Synagogue

Theology Team

Jeffrey Adler, M.Div.
Rabbi, Sha'arey Yeshua Messianic Synagogue, IAMCS

Raymond L. Gannon, M.Div., Th.M., Ph.D., Ph.D.
Director of Messianic Jewish Studies, The King's College and Seminary

Seth Postell, Ph.D.
Professor, Israel College of the Bible

Noel S. Rabinowitz, Th.M., Ph.D.
Associate Professor of Biblical Studies, The King's College

Rich Robinson, M.Div., Ph.D.
Senior Researcher, Jews for Jesus

Eric Tokajer, Th.B.
Rabbi, Brit Ahm Messianic Jewish Synaogue, IAMCS

Theology Team Advisers

Richard E. Averbeck, M.A., M.Div. Ph.D.,
Professor of Old Testament & Semitic Languages,
Trinity Evangelical Divinity School

Daniel Juster, M. Div. M.Div. Th.D.,
Tikkun International Ministries

Craig Keener, M.Div., Ph.D.,
Professor of New Testament, Palmer Seminary of Eastern University

Literary Editor

Glenn Blank, M.A., M.S., Ph.D.
Rabbi, Beit Simcha, IAMCS & Tikkun International

Creative Development Team

Tammy Blenkhorn
Fine Artist—Color Paintings, ybathashem@gmail.com

Dean Drawbaugh
Destiny Image Publishers, Staff Publisher

Daniah Greenberg
Tree of Life Bible, Project Manager

Buck Stephens
Tree of Life Bible, Project Development Consultant

Michael Washer
Fine Artist—Pencil illustrations, graphics and maps
mwmastersdesign.com

www.TreeofLifeBible.org

Board of Reference

FOUNDATION FOR LEADERSHIP AND MESSIANIC EDUCATION
flamefoundation.org

INTERNATIONAL ALLIANCE OF MESSIANIC JEWISH
CONGREGATIONS AND SYNAGOGUES
iamcs.org

JEWISH VOICE MINISTRIES INTERNATIONAL
jewishvoice.org

JEWS FOR JESUS
jewsforjesus.org

JEWISH JEWELS
jewishjewels.org

MESSIANIC DAILY NEWS
messianicdailynews.com

MESSIANIC JEWISH ISRAEL FUND
mjif.org

MESSIANIC JEWISH ALLIANCE OF AMERICA
mjaa.org

MESSIANIC JEWISH RESOURCES INTERNATIONAL
messianicjewish.net

PROMISE KEEPERS & ROAD TO JERUSALEM
promisekeepers.org

SHIVAT TZION MINISTRIES
prophecyrevealed.com

SHORESH DAVID MESSIANIC SYNAGOGUES OF FLORIDA
shoreshdavid.org

SOUNDS OF SHALOM INTERNET RADIO STATION
soundsofshalom.com

TIKKUN MINISTRIES INTERNATIONAL
tikkunministries.org

UNION OF MESSIANIC JEWISH CONGREGATIONS
umjc.org

Foreword

*Hope deferred makes the heart ache, but a longing fulfilled is a **tree of life***
(Proverbs 13:12).

God is love. He created the universe, including humankind. He has always longed to have us love Him the way that He loves us.

God keeps His promises. He started His promise to humankind through Adam and Eve. He put them in a wonderful garden where they walked and talked with their Creator, and were being prepared to eat from the Tree of Life. But Adam and Eve disobeyed God, eating from the wrong tree. So God disciplined them, but also promised to restore them through a "seed of the woman."

Humankind got worse, with murder and idolatry, always inclined toward evil. God continued to hope, preserving Noah's family through the flood, and giving a promise with a rainbow. Generations later, God promised Abraham and Sarah that through them He would create a nation who would inherit the land. Would they love Him?

His promise to Abraham was fulfilled in the birth of Isaac, and through Isaac's son Jacob, the children of Israel were born. The children of Israel sinned against each other and their father, and God humbled them through a great famine and their descendants wound up in Egypt as slaves of Pharaoh. We remember the story of Israel's deliverance at Passover tables around the world. Jews and Christians alike recount the miracles of God's hand freeing His people Israel from the bondage of sin and death.

God's promises to His people are in the *Torah,* the first five books of the Bible. The *Torah* tells the story of how God taught an entire nation, the Israelites, how to live close to Him by obeying His commands and worshiping Him in love. Many times they succeeded; more often, they failed.

God continued to keep His promise to humankind through Moses by creating a way for the children of Israel to find forgiveness for their sins. Through the shedding of blood of sacrificial animals, our ancestors could ask God's forgiveness, wash in water, and then sit down to a meal with God, friends, and family to rejoice and fellowship.

Yet Moses knew that God's longing to restore all humankind to right relationship with Himself would be accomplished in a greater way. Moses promised the people that God would send another prophet, like Moses in word and miraculous deeds, yet even greater in wisdom and power—the Messiah. Just as through Moses God expanded the covenant with Abraham to make more promises to a whole nation, so through Messiah, God would make an even greater covenant with all humanity.

Over many centuries, God spoke to Israel and all humankind through King David, King Solomon, the prophets, as well as through the stories of many lives—both those who revered God and those who rebelled. The heroes of God's story include Joshua, Pinchas, Gideon, Deborah, Ruth, Hezekiah, Josiah, Nehemiah, Esther, and more. God inspired the prophets and priests of Israel to write 39 books for the Hebrew Bible.

Then, the revelation of Scripture fell silent. The people of Israel were waiting expectantly. What would happen next?

In the fullness of time, God sent the Redeemer to His children's children. That Redeemer is *Yeshua*, the Messiah—His given Hebrew name. Some know Him by His Christian name, Jesus, the Christ. Some may not know Him at all. This book introduces Him to you—the descendant of Abraham and Sarah, the Son of David, yet also *Ben-Elohim*, the Son of God. He is the fulfillment of God's longing, the Messiah Israel was expecting. Yet He was and He continues to be a surprise, doing and saying things that our people were not expecting. So His story is always fresh, especially when you read it with a longing to trust God.

John's Eyewitness Account

One of the stories of Yeshua's life is told by His disciple John. That story, commonly called a Gospel, is his eyewitness account of Yeshua's ministry. John, along with over 500 other people, actually saw Yeshua alive after He had risen from the dead. His telling of the story is fascinating. And now Messianic Jews have translated John's story for you to enjoy, absorb, and glean from.

Rest assured that our rigorous translation and vetting process included a team of scholars from the Union of Messianic Jewish Congregations, the International Alliance of Messianic Congregations and Synagogues, Jews for Jesus, and Jewish Voice International Ministries, in cooperation with Tikkun Ministries International and other leading Messianic ministries worldwide. Bringing so many Jewish and Messianic Jewish perspectives together for one project was something of a miracle. Moreover, respected Christian scholars have crosschecked and reviewed the work. Destiny Image Publishing graciously agreed to help fund the development of the manuscript under the direct guidance of the Theology Committee of this Bible project.

Faithfulness to the original text is one key principle for this Book of John and **the Tree of Life Messianic Family Bible.** It is a revision of the public domain American Standard Version of 1901, updated by a Messianic Jewish reading of the Greek text, 27th Nestle Aland Novum Testamentum Graece. The result is a reliable and accurate text that families can enjoy reading together, accessible by all generations.

> Wisdom is a **tree of life** to those who take hold of her, and happy are those who hold her fast (Proverbs 3:18).

For such a momentous task, we asked the Spirit of Messiah to guide us. One great challenge was to maintain a balance between accuracy and readability.

One of the unique features of this version is the vibrant, "in the moment" vividness of this text. You can "hear" John telling his testimony about Messiah as we stick as close to the Greek as possible using the historical present verb tense. This pulls you right into his story!

Another challenge was to remain consistent with our overall Messianic Jewish vision, yet not hardwire slanted doctrinal views into the text. The beauty of having such a diverse team within our Messianic community is that all involved were committed to "do no violence to the text." With unanimous consent, not majority rule, the Lord is blessing our work.

So the Entire World Will Know

For centuries scribes have faithfully preserved the Bible, word for word, in Hebrew, Aramaic, and Greek. If a scribe made a single mistake copying the *Torah*, the whole scroll was considered unfit for use. Before the modern printing press, scribes produced copies on animal skins, and they often illustrated Bibles with beautiful artwork.

In addition to archeological discoveries confirming its historical reliability, one of the most amazing proofs of the Bible's accuracy was found in a cave in the Judean desert, just as the modern state of Israel was born in 1948, when a Bedouin shepherd discovered the Dead Sea Scrolls. Jews who lived in the first century left behind scrolls of most books of the Hebrew Bible. Miraculously, the Word of God has been preserved!

> A soothing tongue is a **tree of life**, but perversion in it crushes the spirit (Proverbs 15:4).

With the invention of the printing press, Bibles became available to own and keep in every home. Before then, only religious leaders could pass Scripture down to people through word of mouth, memorization, and song. Mostly it was read out loud at public gatherings and worship times.

When the United States was colonized, the Bible was an integral part of daily family life. For the next 150 years, it was the mainstay of the family altar at home. With the Bible, children learned how to read, and the Bible became foundational to the moral values, laws, and culture of most Americans, both Christian and Jewish. Yet in recent generations, the prominence of the Family Bible in American life, literacy, and morality has waned. It is time for a Family Bible revolution!

Yeshua—The Tree of Life

We want the whole world to know that it is Jewish to believe in Yeshua, the Jewish Messiah. Yeshua is the Messiah for all who believe—Jew and Gentile alike. We are all one in Messiah's love.

If you are a Jew who is curious about Messiah, this Book of John will help you, with help from the Holy Spirit, to see how Yeshua became the Prophet like Moses, full of glory, grace, and truth. Compare what John says with what the Hebrew Bible says—the footnotes point the way for you.

If you are already a believer in Messiah Yeshua, you are encouraged to share copies of this Gospel of John with others. The seed of the Good News will cause salvation to sprout wherever it is read. Yeshua alone is able to fill an empty heart and rebuild a broken life. Yeshua *is* the Tree of Life.

The Tree of Life Bible

A diverse community of Messianic Jewish and Christian scholars is collaborating to produce the **Tree of Life Messianic Family Bible**. Messianic rabbis, leaders, scholars, artists, professors, psalmists, linguists, writers, parents, and children have come together to work on this new Messianic family version. Over fifteen Messianic organizations have joined together to provide the seed money to begin this project. This Book of John is just the beginning of a revolutionary Bible of truth for Jews and Christians alike.

What makes the **Tree of Life Messianic Family Bible** truly unique? In its leaves are healing for both the Jews and the nations. God does not pit His children against each other.

The **Tree of Life Messianic Family Bible** is for the entire family to read. It includes a small number of Hebrew words that we believe a Messianic Jewish *bar* or *bat mitzvah* should learn how to pronounce and understand. It also contains a glossary of key biblical terms. We italicize the Hebrew words that you can "sound out" using English letters. In this way, you can learn to pronounce Hebrew correctly as you add key words to your biblical vocabulary. Why? Hebrew words often have more layers of meaning than their English counterparts. Learning important Hebrew words helps you understand what the Jewish writers intended when the Spirit inspired them to write.

Here are a few examples:

- *Yeshua* isn't just the Hebrew name for Jesus; the word means "salvation."

- *Shalom* isn't just the Hebrew word for peace. It also means "hello, good-bye, wholeness, completeness, or well-being."

- ADONAI means "LORD." Its use preserves an ancient Jewish tradition. Whenever a Jew encounters the Tetragrammaton—the four-letter name of the Holy One—he or she says ADONAI. With this same reverence, when quoting the holy name from the Hebrew Scriptures, the *Tree of Life Bible* uses the respectful term ADONAI.

Moreover, the **Tree of Life Messianic Family Bible** expresses how Yeshua's fellow Jews would have understood His message. For example, when Yeshua commends people for their faith, He wasn't simply interested in what they thought about Him. After all, even the demons of *satan* recognized that Yeshua is *Ben-Elohim*, and screamed in fear! Yeshua was—and is—looking for disciples who put their trust in Him completely and follow Him without looking back. So the **Tree of Life Messianic Family Bible** sometimes translates the word *believe* as "trust" or "put his trust in" because faith is a decisive action, not simply a momentary thought.

Brand-new pictures, introductions, and headings have been created to restore a more Hebraic understanding. These inspirational portions have been researched and vetted by experts in theology.

*To him who overcomes, I will give the right to eat from the **tree of life*** (Revelation 2:7).

The Overcomers

We know *Yeshua* as *Ben-Elohim*, the Son of God, born of a Jewish virgin, Miriam (Mary). He was raised by Joseph and had siblings, including Jacob and Judah. Jacob and

Judah (commonly called James and Jude) wrote two books of the Bible. This is the same Jacob who led the first community of believers in Jerusalem.

The Sent Ones—the apostles—were all Jews. The Jews were waiting for the promised Redeemer that Moses had spoken about over a thousand years earlier. When Yeshua came proclaiming the Kingdom of God, His fellow Jews were expecting a Messiah who would overthrow the oppressive Romans and exalt Zion as chief of the nations. They weren't expecting a Messiah who would first suffer and die to take away their sins forever. They didn't understand that before they could enter the Kingdom of Heaven, they had to be made new—transformed into people no longer inclined toward evil, but willing to love God with all their hearts, souls, strength, and willing to love their neighbors as themselves.

How many people can say they have consistently kept all of God's commandments? Who has never stolen, lied, coveted? We all need a Lamb of God who washes away our sins and renews a willing spirit. As the prophets foretold, most of *Yeshua's* fellow Jews didn't understand Him. Yet thousands of *Torah*-observant Jews did put their trust in Him, and this remnant turned the world upside down with the Good News of the risen Messiah and Lord!

According to many prophecies in the Hebrew Bible, the Messiah would come not only to deliver the Jewish people, but also to be a light to the nations. One of the first arguments in the New Covenant among the Sent Ones was "what to do" with all the Gentiles who were putting their trust in the Jewish Messiah and being filled with the Spirit. Messiah's followers understood faith in *Yeshua* as a fulfillment of Jewish hopes, not starting a new religion called Christianity.

Then terrible things happened. As *Yeshua* foretold, Jerusalem and the Temple were destroyed when the Romans crushed a Jewish revolt. Jews were driven into exile, and the Roman Empire looked down on them. Christian leaders no longer wanted to be associated with Jews. They forgot that *Yeshua* and His Sent Ones were Jews who loved their fellow Jews and longed for the restoration of Israel. Over time, a chasm formed between Jews and followers of Yeshua. Church leaders developed the idea that since the Jews had rejected Yeshua, God had rejected the Jews, transferring His covenant promises to the Church and leaving Israel with the curses. Tragically, walls formed between Jews and Christians, with Jews herded into ghettos.

Yet the Bible insists that God is not a man who changes His mind. God is the same yesterday, today, and forever, and He is faithful to His covenants forever. God aches for the restoration of Israel and the fulfillment of all His promises. God longs for the day when Messiah will return and establish His Kingdom upon the earth. God longs to restore all people to right understanding of His Word, so that He can restore us all in His Kingdom.

Yeshua—the Jewish Messiah

There have always been Jewish believers in *Yeshua*. Since the resurrection of the modern state of Israel, the numbers have multiplied—first in the United States, then around the world, and now in Israel. Moreover, there is an understanding growing between Messianic Jews and their Christian brothers that the time for Messiah's return is growing near.

*The fruit of the righteous is a **tree of life**, and he who is wise wins souls* (Proverbs 11:30).

As you read this Book of John from the ***Tree of Life Messianic Family Bible***, you will see how *Yeshua* observed *Shabbat*, Passover, and *Sukkot* (Tabernacles) with His people, and even *Hanukkah* (the Feast of Dedication) in Jerusalem. *Yeshua* teaches directly from the *Torah*—referenced for you in the footnotes. You can show any Jewish friend exactly what *Yeshua* teaches from the Hebrew Bible.

Many modern-day Christians recognize the value of rediscovering the Jewish roots of their faith. Messianic Jews are growing in numbers and scholarship. The middle wall of partition is crumbling, and the Spirit of God is restoring our unity and teaching us that our diversity is our strength, not a weakness. The time to favor Zion is now.

Tree of Life Messianic Family Bible Production Details

Instead of including written commentary or using proof texting techniques, we have created brand-new introductions and headings to restore a more Hebraic understanding. These have also been researched and vetted by experts in theology.

This Book of John has four new pieces of Messianic Jewish art! When the full ***Tree of Life Messianic Family Bible*** is completed, there will be more than 60 color and black/white images that bring to life this amazing story. Because art is in the eye of the beholder, remember that these are images of what the artist believes was happening at the time. This is the first Bible to have artwork drawn by Messianic Jews in our century—very unique and special.

From a Jewish perspective, in an honest attempt to include artwork without falling into the trap of creating idolatrous images, we made the following concessions. We created highly detailed black and white images and more stylized pictures that will be featured in full color when the entire Bible is finished. By not showing finely detailed art in color, we hope you will finish the picture with your own interpretation. In fact, all but one picture of Messiah, *Yeshua*, does not show His entire face since we don't know exactly what He looked like.

We did, however, make one exception on purpose. We showed *Yeshua's* whole face—after the resurrection—when Peter jumps out of the boat to meet Him. Why the one exception? Because *Yeshua's* face has been illustrated by hundreds of artists over the centuries as anything but Jewish! We want to allow another perspective into the biblical thought arena on the Jewish lineage of our Messiah. We also include women in the artwork—another important aspect.

As an extra measure of grace to those who may not prefer the artistic renderings, feel free to remove it, as the reverse of that page was left blank on purpose. Likewise, we invite you to write to us on the Web (see the following e-mail address) and let us know whether or not you think we should include the picture of Yeshua's full face in the *Tree of Life Messianic Family Bible*.

A Worldwide, Life-Changing Project

Stay in touch with the *Tree of Life Messianic Family Bible* project.

Foreword

Anticipated publication dates for the *Tree of Life Messianic Family Bible* components:

Gospel of John, July 2010

Gospels of Matthew, Mark, Luke (and John), January 2011

New Covenant, July 2011

Torah (Chumash), July 2012

Tree of Life Messianic Family Bible, July 2013

New maps and helps pages are still under construction. We welcome your feedback and support. Visit our Web site: www.TreeofLifeBible.org. Future installments of the New Covenant and the *Tree of Life Bible* will be available in "apps" for mobile devices.

We encourage you to e-mail us at:

spreadtheword@messianicfamilybible.org.

John

Introduction

John, one of the twelve original apostles, the Sent Ones, wrote this fourth Gospel, or *Besorah*. He was one of the sons of Zebedee, along with Jacob. Written in a style completely different than the other three, it dates from the end of the first century (probably about 90–95 C.E.). Writing many years after *Yeshua's* resurrection, John includes in his account the kinds of deep insights one would expect of a young student who was present with *Yeshua* and has now grown into a mature and wise sage.

At one time, John was believed to be the least Jewish of the gospels. Now that scholars have learned more about first-century Judaism (including the discovery and study of the Dead Sea Scrolls), John is recognized to be very Jewish indeed. Other Jewish writers of this period also attribute divinity to the Word (*Logos* in Greek, *Memra* in Aramaic). Some of the speeches of *Yeshua* in John resemble a rabbinic commentary or *midrash*, and a wealth of references point to the Jewish traditions and institutions dating from the time of the *Tanakh*—Jacob's ladder, *Shabbat, Sukkot, Hanukkah, Pesach*, the serpent in the wilderness, and *manna*—all make their appearance here.

John was written at a time when intra-Jewish conflicts over *Yeshua* and the claims of his followers were running high. In some instances, Jewish believers in *Yeshua* were no longer welcome in the synagogues. In this context, some believe that John wrote to Jewish nonbelievers to answer the question, "Who is the Messiah?" John's answer, of course, is *Yeshua*, seen as both human and divine in nature, the Son of God, or *Ben-Elohim*. Others think it was written primarily to encourage Jewish believers to pursue a deeper, persevering level of faith in light of the opposition. Either way, the audience appears to be largely Jewish. John works both to encourage those who believe in *Yeshua* and to lead to faith those who do not yet put their trust in Him. *Yeshua's* words and deeds reveal who He is: the Word of God who tabernacled among us, the Lamb of God who takes away the sin of the world, the Light of the World, and much more.

The Word of God Becomes Flesh (1:1)
John's Witness to Israel's Leaders (1:19)
Behold, the Lamb of God (1:29)
Yeshua's First *Talmidim* (1:35)
Talmidim Offer Witness to *Yeshua* (1:43)

The Miracle of Water to Wine (2:1)
Yeshua Purges the Holy Temple (2:12)
A Jewish Truth-Seeker Comes to *Yeshua* (3:1)
God's Love Is Revealed in *Yeshua* (3:9)
The Living Word Is the Source of Life (3:22)

1 The Word of God Becomes Flesh

[1]In the beginning was the Word.[i] The Word was with God, and the Word was God. [2]He was with God in the beginning. [3]All things were made through Him, and apart from Him nothing was made that has come into being. [4]In Him was life, and the life was the light of men. [5]The light shines in the darkness, and the darkness has not overpowered it.

[6]There came a man sent from God, whose name was John. [7]He came as a witness to testify about the light, so that through him everyone might believe. [8]He was not the light, but he came to bear witness concerning the light. [9]The true light, coming into the world, gives light to every man.

[10]He was in the world, and the world was made through Him; but the world did not know Him. [11]He came to His own, but His own did not welcome Him. [12]But whoever did welcome Him, those trusting in His name, to these He gave the right to become children of God. [13]They were born not of a bloodline, nor of human desire, nor of man's will, but of God. [14]And the Word became flesh and tabernacled among us. We looked upon His glory,[ii] the glory of the One and only from the Father, full of grace and truth.

[15]John testifies about Him. He cried out, saying, "This is He of whom I said, 'The One who comes after me is above me, because He existed before me.'" [16]Out of His fullness, we have all received grace on top of grace. [17]*Torah* was given through Moses; grace and truth came through *Yeshua* the Messiah. [18]No one has ever seen God; but the one and only God,[iii] in the Father's embrace, has made Him known.

John's Witness to Israel's Leaders

[19]This is John's testimony, when the Judean leaders sent priests and Levites from Jerusalem to ask him, "Who are you?"

[20]He openly admitted and did not deny; he admitted, "I am not the Messiah."

[21]"What then? Are you Elijah?" they asked him.

"I am not," said John.

"Are you the Prophet?"

"No," he answered.

[22]So they said to him, "Who are you? Give us an answer for those who sent us. What do you say about yourself?"

[23]He said, "I am 'the voice of one crying in the wilderness, "Make straight the way of ADONAI!"'[iv] as the prophet Isaiah said."

[24]Now those sent were from the Pharisees. [25]They asked him, "If you're not the Messiah, Elijah, or the Prophet, why then are you immersing?"

[26]"I immerse in water," John answered. "Among you stands One you do not know, [27]coming after me, whose sandals I'm not worthy to untie." [28]These things happened in Bethany beyond the Jordan, where John was immersing.

Behold, the Lamb of God

[29]The next day, John sees *Yeshua* coming to him and says, "Behold, the Lamb[v] of God who takes away the sin of the world! [30]This is the One about whom I told you, 'He who comes after me is above me, because He was before me.' [31]I didn't know Him, but I came immersing with water so that He might be revealed to Israel."

[32]Then John testified, "I've seen the Spirit coming down like a dove out of heaven, and it remained on Him. [33]I didn't know Him; but the One who sent me to immerse in water said to me, 'The One on whom you see the Spirit coming down and remaining, this is the One who immerses in the Holy Spirit.' [34]And

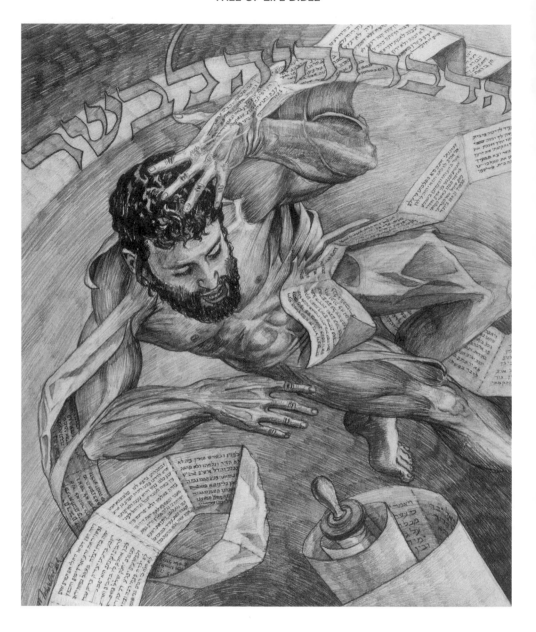

The Word Became Flesh   John 1:1-14

"And the Word became flesh and tabernacled among us . . ." —John 1:14

I have seen and testified that this is *Ben-Elohim*."

Yeshua's First *Talmidim*

³⁵Again the next day, John was standing with two of his disciples ³⁶and watched *Yeshua* walking by. He said, "Behold, the Lamb of God!" ³⁷The two disciples heard him say this, and they followed *Yeshua*.

³⁸*Yeshua* turned around and saw them following. He said to them, "What are you looking for?"

They said to Him, "Rabbi" (which is translated Teacher), "where are you staying?"

³⁹"Come and see," *Yeshua* tells them. So they came and saw where He was staying, and they spent that day with Him. It was about the tenth hour.

⁴⁰ Andrew, the brother of Simon Peter, was one of the two who heard John speak and followed *Yeshua*. ⁴¹First he finds his own brother Simon and tells him, "We've found the Messiah!" (which is translated Anointed One).

⁴²Andrew brought Simon to *Yeshua*. *Yeshua* looked at him and said, "You are Simon, son of John. You shall be called *Kefa* (which is translated Peter)."

Talmidim Offer Witness to *Yeshua*

⁴³The next day, *Yeshua* decided to go to the Galilee. He finds Philip and says to him, "Follow Me!" ⁴⁴Now Philip was from Bethsaida, the same town as Andrew and Peter.

⁴⁵Philip finds Nathanael and tells him, "We've found the One that Moses in the *Torah*, and also the prophets, wrote about — *Yeshua* of Nazareth, the son of Joseph!"

⁴⁶"Nazareth!" Nathanael answered. "Can anything good come from there?"

Philip said to him, "Come and see."

⁴⁷*Yeshua* saw Nathanael coming toward Him. He said, "Look, a true Israelite! There's nothing false in him."

⁴⁸Nathanael said to Him, "How do you know me?"

Yeshua answered, "Before Philip called you, when you were under the fig tree, I saw you."

⁴⁹"Rabbi," Nathanael answered, "You are *Ben-Elohim*! You are the King of Israel!"ⁿⁱ

⁵⁰"Because I told you that I saw you under the fig tree, you believe?" *Yeshua* replied to him. "You will see greater things than that!" ⁵¹And He said, "Amen! Amen! I tell you, you will see heaven opened and the angels of God going up and coming down on the Son of Man!"ᵛⁱⁱ

2 The Miracle of Water to Wine

¹On the third day, there was a wedding at Cana in the Galilee. *Yeshua*'s mother was there, ²and *Yeshua* and His disciples were also invited to the wedding. ³When the wine ran out, *Yeshua*'s mother said to Him, "They don't have any wine!"

⁴*Yeshua* said to her, "Madam, what does this have to do with you and Me? My hour hasn't yet come."

⁵His mother said to the servants, "Do whatever He tells you."

⁶Now there were six stone jars, used for the Jewish ritual of purification, each holding two to three measures.ᵛⁱⁱⁱ ⁷*Yeshua* said to them, "Fill the jars with water!" So they filled them up to the top. ⁸Then He said to them, "Take some water out, and give it to the master of ceremonies." And they brought it.

⁹Now the master of ceremonies didn't know where it had come from, but the servants who had drawn the water knew. As the master of ceremonies tasted the water that had become wine, he calls the bridegroom ¹⁰and says to him, "Everyone brings out the good wine first, and whenever they are drunk,

then the worse. But you've reserved the good wine until now!" [11]Yeshua did this, the first of the signs, in Cana of the Galilee. And He revealed His glory, and His disciples believed in Him.

Yeshua Purges the Holy Temple

[12]After this Yeshua went down to Capernaum with His mother, brothers,[ix] and disciples, and they stayed there a few days. [13]The Jewish feast of Passover was near, so Yeshua went up to Jerusalem. [14]In the Temple, He found the merchants selling oxen, sheep, and doves; also the moneychangers sitting there. [15]Then He made a whip of cords and drove them all out of the Temple, both the sheep and oxen. He dumped out the coins of the moneychangers and flipped their tables. [16]To those selling doves, He said, "Get these things out of here! Stop making My Father's house a marketplace!" [17]His disciples remembered that it is written, "Zeal for your House will consume Me!"[x]

[18]The Judean leaders responded, "What sign do You show us, since You are doing these things?"

[19]"Destroy this Temple," Yeshua answered them, "and in three days I will raise it up."

[20]The Judean leaders then said to Him, "Forty-six years this Temple was being built, and You will raise it up in three days?" [21]But He was talking about the Temple of His body. [22]So after He was raised from the dead, His disciples remembered that He was talking about this. Then they believed the Scripture and the word that Yeshua had spoken.

[23]Now when He was in Jerusalem for the Passover, during the feast, many believed in His name, seeing the signs He was doing. [24]But Yeshua did not entrust Himself to them, because He knew all men. [25]He didn't need anyone to testify about man, for He knew what was in man.

3 A Jewish Truth-Seeker Comes to Yeshua

[1]Now there was a man, a Pharisee named Nicodemus, a ruler of the Jews. [2]He came to Yeshua at night and said, "Rabbi, we know that You, a teacher, have come from God. For no one can perform these signs that You do unless God is with Him!"

[3]Yeshua answered him, "Amen! Amen! I tell you, unless one is born from above,[xi] he cannot see the kingdom of God."

[4]"How can a man be born when he is old?" Nicodemus said to Him. "He cannot enter his mother's womb a second time and be born, can he?"

[5]Yeshua answered, "Amen! Amen! I tell you, unless one is born of water and spirit,[xii] he cannot enter the kingdom of God. [6]What's born of the flesh is flesh, and what's born of the Spirit is spirit. [7]Don't be surprised that I said to you, 'You all must be born from above.' [8]The wind blows where it wishes and you hear its sound, but you don't know where it comes from or where it goes. So it is with everyone born of the Spirit."

God's Love Is Revealed in Yeshua

[9]"How can these things happen?" Nicodemus said.

[10]Yeshua answered him, "You're a teacher of Israel and you don't understand these things? [11]Amen! Amen! I tell you, We speak about what We know and testify about what We have seen. Yet you all do not accept Our testimony! [12]If you don't believe the earthly things I said to you, how will you believe when I tell you about heavenly things? [13]No one has gone up into heaven except the One who came down from heaven—the Son of Man. [14]Just as Moses lifted up the snake in the desert,[xiii] so the Son of Man must

be lifted up, ¹⁵so that whoever believes in Him may have eternal life!

¹⁶"For God so loved the world that He gave His one and only Son, that whoever believes in Him shall not perish but have eternal life. ¹⁷God did not send the Son into the world to judge the world, but in order that the world might be saved through Him. ¹⁸The one who believes in Him is not judged; but whoever doesn't believe has been judged already, because he hasn't put his trust in the name of the one and only Son of God.

¹⁹"Now this is the judgment, that the light has come into the world and men loved the darkness instead of the light,ˣⁱᵛ because their deeds were evil. ²⁰For everyone who does evil hates the light and does not come to the light, so that their deeds will not be exposed. ²¹But whoever practices the truth comes to the light, so that it may be made known that his deeds have been accomplished in God."

The Living Word Is the Source of Life

²²Afterwards, *Yeshua* and His disciples came to the land of Judea. There He was staying with them and immersing. ²³Now John also was immersing at Aenon near Salim, because much water was there and many were coming and being immersed; ²⁴for John had not yet been thrown into prison.

²⁵Now an argument came up between John's disciples and a Judean concerning purification. ²⁶They came to John and said, "Rabbi, the One who was with you beyond the Jordan, the One you testified about—look, He is immersing, and all are coming to Him!"

²⁷John answered, "A man can receive nothing unless it has been given to him from heaven. ²⁸You yourselves testify that I said, 'I'm not the Messiah,' but rather, 'I am sent before Him.' ²⁹The one who has the bride is the bridegroom, but the best man rejoices when he stands and hears the bridegroom's voice. So now my joy is complete! ³⁰He must increase, while I must decrease.

³¹"The One who comes from above is above all. The one who is from the earth is of the earth, and of the earth he speaks. The One who comes from heaven is above all. ³²And what He has seen and heard, He testifies to that; yet no one receives His testimony. ³³Whoever receives His testimony has certified that God is true.

³⁴The One whom God has sent speaks the words of God, for God gives the Spirit without limit. ³⁵The Father loves the Son and has given everything into His hand. ³⁶He who trusts in the Son has eternal life. He who doesn't obey the Son will not see life, but the wrath of God remains on him."

4 Yeshua Offers Living Water

¹Now *Yeshua* knew that the Pharisees heard that He was making and immersing more disciples than John. ²(Although *Yeshua* Himself was not immersing, His disciples were.) ³So He left Judea and went back again to the Galilee.

⁴But He needed to pass through Samaria. ⁵So He comes to a Samaritan town called Sychar, near the plot of landˣᵛ that Jacob gave to his son Joseph. ⁶Now Jacob's well was there. So *Yeshua*, exhausted from the journey, was sitting by the well. It was midday.ˣᵛⁱ

⁷A Samaritan woman comes to draw water. "Give me a drink," *Yeshua* said to her, ⁸for His disciples had gone away to the town to buy food.

⁹Then the Samaritan woman said to Him, "How is it that You, a Jew, ask me, a Samaritan woman, for a drink?" (For Jews don't deal with Samaritans.)

[10]*Yeshua* answered her, "If you knew the gift of God, and who it is who is saying to you, 'Give Me a drink,' you would've asked Him, and He would've given you living water."

[11]"Sir," the woman said to Him, "You don't have a bucket, and the well is deep. Then from where do You get this living water? [12]You're not greater than our father Jacob, are You? He gave us this well. He drank out of it himself, with his sons and his cattle."

[13]*Yeshua* answered, "Everyone who drinks from this water will get thirsty again. [14]But whoever drinks of the water that I will give him shall never be thirsty again! The water that I give him will become a fountain of water within him, springing up to eternal life!"

[15]"Sir," the woman said to Him, "give me this water, so I won't get thirsty or have to come all the way here to draw water."

[16]He said to her, "Go call your husband, and then come back here."

[17]"I don't have a husband," the woman answered.

Yeshua said to her, "You've said it right, 'I have no husband,' [18]for you have had five husbands. And the man you have now isn't your husband. This you've spoken truthfully!"

[19]"Sir," the woman said to Him, "I see that You are a prophet! [20]Our fathers worshiped on this mountain, but you all say that the place where we must worship is in Jerusalem."

[21]*Yeshua* said to her, "Woman, believe Me, an hour is coming when you will worship the Father neither on this mountain nor in Jerusalem. [22]You worship what you do not know; we worship what we know, for salvation is from the Jews. [23]But an hour is coming—it is here now—when the true worshipers will worship the Father in Spirit and truth, for the Father is seeking such people as His worshipers. [24]God is Spirit, and those who worship Him must worship in Spirit and truth."

[25]The woman said to Him, "I know that Messiah is coming (He who is called the Anointed One[xvii]). When He comes, He will explain everything to us."

[26]*Yeshua* says to her, "I am—the One who is speaking to you."

The Ready Harvest of Eternal Life

[27]And at this moment, His disciples came back. They were amazed that He was speaking with a woman. Yet no one said, "What do You want?" or "Why are You speaking with her?"

[28]So the woman left her water jar and went back to the town. She tells the people, [29]"Come see a man who told me everything I ever did! He couldn't be the Messiah, could He?" [30]The people left the town and began coming to Him.

[31]Meanwhile, the disciples were pressing Him, "Rabbi, eat!"

[32]But He said to them, "I have food to eat that you know nothing about."

[33]So the disciples were saying to each other, "No one brought Him food to eat, did they?"

[34]*Yeshua* tells them, "My food is to do the will of the One who sent Me and to accomplish His work. [35]Don't you say, 'Four more months, and then comes the harvest'? Look, I tell you, lift up your eyes and look at the fields! They are white and ready for harvest.

[36]"The reaper receives a reward and gathers fruit for eternal life, so that the sower and reaper may rejoice together. [37]For the saying is true, 'One sows and another reaps.' [38]I sent you to reap what you haven't worked for. Others have worked hard, and you have joined in their work."

[39]Many of the Samaritans from that town put their trust in Him because of the word of the woman testifying, "He told me everything that I ever did!" [40]So when the Samaritans came to Him, they kept asking Him to stay with them. He stayed there two days, [41]and many more believed because of His word. [42]They kept telling the woman, "It's no longer because of your words that we believe. We've heard for ourselves! Now we

know that this really is the Savior of the world!"

Healing the Dying Son

⁴³After the two days, He went on from there into the Galilee. ⁴⁴Now *Yeshua* Himself had testified that a prophet has no honor in his own country. ⁴⁵But when He came into the Galilee, they welcomed Him. For they had seen all He had done at the feast in Jerusalem, since they also had gone up to celebrate.

⁴⁶So He went again to Cana of the Galilee, where He had turned the water into wine. Now there was a nobleman whose son was sick in Capernaum. ⁴⁷When he heard that *Yeshua* had come from Judea to the Galilee, he went to Him. And he was begging *Yeshua* to come down and heal his son, who was about to die.

⁴⁸Then *Yeshua* said to him, "Unless you people see signs and wonders, you'll never believe!"

⁴⁹The nobleman said to Him, "Sir, come down before my child dies!"

⁵⁰*Yeshua* tells him, "Go! Your son lives!"

The man believed the word that *Yeshua* said to him and started off. ⁵¹While on his way down, his servants met him, saying that his son was living. ⁵²So he asked them the hour when the boy began to get better. They said, "The fever left him yesterday at about the seventh hour."ˣᵛⁱⁱⁱ

⁵³Then the father realized that it was the same hour *Yeshua* said to him, "Your son lives!" And he believed, along with his whole household. ⁵⁴This is the second sign *Yeshua* performed when He came from Judea into the Galilee.

5 Healing the Invalid on *Shabbat*

¹After this there was a Jewish feast, and *Yeshua* went up to Jerusalem. ²Now in Jerusalem there's a pool by the sheep gate, called Bethzatha in Aramaic,ˣⁱˣ which has five porches. ³In these a crowd of invalids was lying around—blind, lame, disabled.ˣˣ

⁵Now a certain man had been an invalid there for thirty-eight years. ⁶Seeing him lying there and knowing he had been that way a long time, *Yeshua* said to him, "Do you want to get well?"

⁷The invalid answered Him, "Sir, I have nobody to put me into the pool when the water is stirred up. While I'm trying to get in, somebody else steps down before me!"

⁸*Yeshua* tells him, "Get up! Pick up your mat and walk!"

⁹Immediately, the man was healed! He took up his mat and started walking around. Now that day was *Shabbat*, ¹⁰so Judean leaders were saying to the man who was healed, "It's *Shabbat*! It's not permitted for you to carry your mat."

¹¹But he answered them, "The man who made me well told me, 'Pick up your mat and walk.'"

¹²They asked him, "Who is the man who told you, 'Pick up your mat and walk'?" ¹³But the man who had been healed didn't know who it was, for *Yeshua* had slipped away into the crowd in that place.

¹⁴Afterwards, *Yeshua* finds him in the Temple. He said to him, "Look, you've been healed! Stop sinning, so nothing worse happens to you." ¹⁵The man left and told the Judean leaders that it was *Yeshua* who had made him well.

Yeshua Is God's Life Agent

¹⁶Because *Yeshua* was doing these things on *Shabbat*, the Judean leaders started persecuting Him. ¹⁷But *Yeshua* said to them, "My Father is still working, and I also am working." ¹⁸So for this reason the Judean leaders were trying even harder to kill Him. Not only was He ignoring *Shabbat*, but He also was calling God His own Father, making Himself equal with God.

[19]Therefore *Yeshua* answered them, "Amen! Amen! I tell you, the Son cannot do anything by Himself. He can do only what He sees the Father doing. Whatever the Father does, the Son does likewise. [20]For the Father loves the Son and shows Him everything He does. He will show Him even greater works than these, so that you will be amazed. [21]For just as the Father raises the dead and gives them life, so also the Son gives life to whomever He wants. [22]The Father doesn't judge anyone, but has handed over all judgment to the Son [23]so that all should honor the Son, just as they honor the Father. Whoever doesn't honor the Son doesn't honor the Father who sent Him.

[24]"Amen! Amen! I tell you, whoever hears My word, and trusts the One who sent Me, has eternal life and does not come into judgment; but he has passed over from death into life. [25]Amen! Amen! I tell you, an hour is coming and is now here, when the dead will hear the voice of *Ben-Elohim.* Those who hear will live! [26]For just as the Father has life in Himself, so also He has granted the Son to have life in Himself. [27]Also He has given the Son authority to judge, because He is the Son of Man.

[28]"Don't be amazed at this, for an hour is coming when all who are in their graves will hear His voice [29]and come out![xxi] Those who have done good will come to a resurrection of life, and those who have done evil will come to a resurrection of judgment. [30]I can do nothing on My own. Just as I hear, I judge; and My judgment is just, for I do not seek My own will, but the will of the One who sent Me."

The Father Testifies about *Yeshua*

[31]"If I testify about Myself, My witness isn't valid. [32]There's another who testifies about Me, and I know that the testimony He gives is true. [33]You have sent to John, and he has testified to the truth. [34]I do not receive the testimony of man, but I say these things so that you may be saved. [35]He was the lamp that was burning and shining, and you wanted to rejoice for a while in his light.

[36]"But the testimony I have is greater than that from John. The works the Father has given Me to finish—the very works I am doing—testify about Me, that the Father has sent Me. [37]And the Father who sent Me has testified concerning Me. You have never heard His voice nor seen His form. [38]Nor do you have His Word living in you, because you do not trust the One He sent. [39]You search the Scriptures because you suppose that in them you have eternal life. It is these that testify about Me. [40]Yet you're not willing to come to Me so that you may have life!

[41]"I do not accept glory from men. [42]But I know you, that you do not have the love of God in yourselves. [43]I have come in My Father's name, and you do not accept Me. But if another comes in his own name, you will accept him. [44]How can you believe, when you accept glory from one another and you do not seek the glory that comes from God alone?

[45]"Do not think that I will accuse you before the Father. The one who accuses you is Moses, in whom you have put your hope. [46]For if you were believing Moses, you would believe Me, because he wrote about Me. [47]But since you don't believe his writings, how will you believe My words?"[xxii]

6 New *Manna* in the Wilderness

[1]Afterward, *Yeshua* went away to the other side of the Sea of Galilee, also known as the Sea of Tiberias. [2]A large crowd kept following Him, because they were watching the signs He was performing on the sick. [3]Then *Yeshua* went up the mountainside and sat down

there with His disciples. ⁴Passover, the Jewish feast, was near.

⁵Lifting up His eyes and seeing a large crowd coming to Him, *Yeshua* said to Philip, "Where will we buy bread so that these may eat?" ⁶Now *Yeshua* was saying this to test him, for He knew what He was about to do.

⁷Philip answered Him, "Two hundred denarii[xxiii] isn't enough to buy bread for them, for each one to get a small bite!"

⁸One of His disciples, Andrew, Simon Peter's brother, said to Him, ⁹"There's a boy here who has five barley loaves and two fish, but what's that for so many?"

¹⁰*Yeshua* said, "Make the people recline." There was much grass in the area. So the men reclined, about five thousand in number. ¹¹Then *Yeshua* picked up the loaves. And having given thanks, He distributed bread to everyone who was reclining. He did the same with the fish, as much as they wanted.

¹²When the people were full, *Yeshua* said to His disciples, "Gather up the leftovers, so nothing is wasted." ¹³So they gathered them and filled twelve baskets with broken pieces from the five barley loaves, which were left over by those who had finished eating.

¹⁴When the people saw the sign that *Yeshua* performed, they began to say, "This is most certainly the Prophet who is to come into the world!"[xxiv] ¹⁵Realizing that they were about to come and seize Him by force to make Him king, *Yeshua* withdrew again to the mountain, Himself alone.

The Savior on the Sea

¹⁶Now when evening came, *Yeshua's* disciples went down to the sea. ¹⁷Getting into a boat, they set out to cross the *sea* toward Capernaum. By now it had become dark, and still *Yeshua* had not come to them. ¹⁸A great wind began to blow, arousing the sea.

¹⁹After they had rowed about twenty-five or thirty stadia,[xxv] they catch sight of *Yeshua* walking on the sea, approaching the boat. They were terrified! ²⁰But *Yeshua* says to them, "I am. Don't be afraid!"[xxvi] ²¹Then they wanted to take Him into the boat; and right away, the boat reached the shore where they were headed.

Yeshua Is the Bread from Heaven

²²The next day, the crowd remaining on the other side of the sea realized that no other boat had been there except the one, and that *Yeshua* hadn't gone into the boat with His disciples, but that His disciples had gone away alone. ²³Some other boats from Tiberias came close to the place where they had eaten the bread after the Master had given thanks. ²⁴So when the crowd realized that neither *Yeshua* nor His disciples were there, they got into the boats and set off for Capernaum to find Him. ²⁵When they found Him on the other side of the sea, they said, "Rabbi, when did You get here?"

²⁶*Yeshua* responded to them, "Amen! Amen! I tell you, you seek Me not because you saw signs, but because you ate all the bread and were filled. ²⁷Don't work for food that spoils, but for the food that endures to eternal life, which the Son of Man will give to you. For on Him, God the Father has put the seal of approval."

²⁸Then they said to Him, "What shall we do to perform the works of God?"

²⁹*Yeshua* answered them, "This is the work of God, to trust in the One He sent."

³⁰So they said to Him, "Then what sign do You perform, so that we may see and believe You? What work do You do? ³¹Our fathers ate the manna in the wilderness; as it is written, 'Out of heaven He gave them bread to eat.'"[xxvii]

³²*Yeshua* answered them, "Amen! Amen! I tell you, it isn't Moses who has given you bread from heaven, but My Father gives you the true bread from heaven. ³³For the bread of God is the One

coming down from heaven and giving life to the world."

34So they said to Him, "Sir, give us this bread from now on!"

35*Yeshua* said to them, "I am the bread of life! Whoever comes to Me will never be hungry, and whoever believes in Me will never be thirsty. 36But I told you that you have seen Me, yet you do not believe. 37Everyone the Father gives Me will come to Me, and anyone coming to Me I will never reject. 38For I have come down from heaven not to do My own will but the will of the One who sent Me.

39"Now this is the will of the One who sent Me, that I lose not one of all He has given Me, but raise each one on the last day. 40For this is the will of My Father, that everyone who sees the Son and trusts in Him may have eternal life; and I will raise him up on the last day."

41Some of the Judeans[xxviii] started to grumble about Him, because He said, "I am the bread that came down from heaven." 42They were saying, "Isn't this *Yeshua* the son of Joseph, whose father and mother we know? How can He now say, 'I have come down from heaven'?"

43*Yeshua* answered, "Stop grumbling among yourselves! 44No one can come to Me unless My Father who sent Me draws him, and I will raise him up on the last day. 45It is written in the Prophets, 'They will all be taught by God.'[xxix] Everyone who has listened and learned from the Father comes to Me. 46Not that anyone has seen the Father except the One who is from God; He has seen the Father.

47"Amen! Amen! I tell you, he who believes has eternal life. 48I am the bread of life. 49Your fathers ate the manna in the desert, yet they died. 50This is the bread that comes down from heaven, so that anybody may eat and not die. 51I am the living bread, which came down from heaven. If anyone eats this bread, he will live forever. This bread is My flesh, which I will give for the life of the world."

52Then the Jews began arguing with one another, "How can this man give us His flesh to eat?"

53So *Yeshua* said to them, "Amen! Amen! I tell you, unless you eat the flesh of the Son of Man and drink His blood, you have no life in yourselves. 54He who eats My flesh and drinks My blood has eternal life, and I will raise him up on the last day.

55"For My flesh is real food and My blood is real drink. 56He who eats My flesh and drinks My blood abides in Me, and I in him. 57Just as the living Father sent Me and I live because of the Father, so the one who eats of Me will also live because of Me. 58This is the bread that came down from heaven—not like the bread your fathers ate and then died. He who eats this bread will live forever."

59He said these things while teaching at the synagogue in Capernaum.

Painful Rejection of Spiritual Life

60So when many of His disciples heard this, they said, "This is a hard teaching. Who can listen to it?"

61But *Yeshua* knew His disciples were murmuring, so He said to them, "Does this offend you? 62Then what if you see the Son of Man going back up to the place where He was before? 63It is the Spirit who gives life; the flesh is of no benefit. The words I have spoken to you are Spirit and are life! 64Yet some of you do not trust." *Yeshua* knew from the beginning who were the ones who didn't trust and which one would betray Him.

65Then He told them, "For this reason I've told you that no one can come to Me unless it has been granted to him by the Father." 66From this time, many of His disciples left and quit walking with Him.

67So *Yeshua* said to the twelve, "You don't want to leave also, do you?"

68Simon Peter answered Him, "Lord, to whom shall we go? You have the words of eternal life! 69We have trusted and have come to know that you are the Holy One of God."

[70]*Yeshua* answered them, "Didn't I choose you, the twelve? Yet one of you is the adversary!" [71]Now He was speaking of Judah, the son of Simon of Kriot; for he, one of the twelve, was about to betray Him.

7 Anticipating Hostility at *Sukkot*

[1]After these events, *Yeshua* was walking about in the Galilee. He didn't want to walk in Judea, because the Judean leaders wanted to kill Him. [2]Now the Jewish Feast of Tabernacles[xxx] was near. [3]Therefore, His brothers said to Him, "Leave here and go to Judea, so Your disciples also may see the works You are doing. [4]No one who wants to be well known does everything in secret. If You are doing these things, show Yourself to the world!" [5]For not even His brothers were trusting in Him.

[6]Therefore *Yeshua* said to them, "My time has not yet come, but your time is always ready. [7]The world cannot hate you, but it hates Me because I testify that its works are evil. [8]You go on up to the Feast. I'm not going to this Feast, because My time hasn't yet fully come." [9]After saying these things, He stayed in the Galilee.

[10]But after His brothers went to the Feast, He also went, not openly but secretly. [11]Then the Judean leaders were searching for Him at the Feast and kept asking, "Where is that man?" [12]There was a lot of murmuring about Him in the crowds. Some were saying, "He's a good man." But others were saying, "Not so! He leads the people astray." [13]Yet no one spoke openly about Him for fear of the Judean leaders.

Yeshua Teaches in the Temple

[14]About halfway through the Feast, Yeshua went up to the Temple and began teaching. [15]Then the Judean leaders were amazed, saying, "How does this man know so much, having never been taught?"[xxxi]

[16]*Yeshua* answered, "My teaching is not from Me, but from Him who sent Me. [17]If anyone wants to do His will, he will know whether My teaching comes from God or it is Myself speaking. [18]Whoever speaks from himself seeks his own glory; but He who seeks the glory of the One who sent Him, He is true and there is no unrighteousness in Him. [19]Hasn't Moses given you the *Torah*? Yet none of you keeps it. Why are you trying to kill Me?"

[20]The crowd answered, "You have a demon! Who's trying to kill you?"

[21]*Yeshua* answered, "I did one good work, and all of you are amazed. [22]Because Moses has given you circumcision (though it's not from Moses, but from the patriarchs), you circumcise a man on *Shabbat*. [23]If a man receives circumcision on *Shabbat* so that the *Torah* of Moses may not be broken, why are you angry that I healed a man's whole body on *Shabbat*? [24]Do not judge by appearance, but judge righteously."

[25]Then some of the people from Jerusalem were saying, "Isn't this the man they're trying to kill? [26]Look, He speaks openly and they're saying nothing to Him. Can it be that the leaders know He is the Messiah? [27]But we know where this man is from. But the Messiah, whenever He may come, no one knows where He is from."

[28]Then, while teaching in the Temple courts, *Yeshua* cried out, "You know both who I am and where I'm from! I have not come on My own, but the One who sent me is true. You do not know Him, [29]but I know Him because I am from Him and He sent Me."

[30]Then they were trying to seize Him; but no one laid a hand on Him, because His hour had not yet come. [31]Yet many from the crowd believed in Him and were saying, "When the Messiah comes, He

won't perform more signs than this man has, will He?" ³²The Pharisees heard people in the crowd murmuring these things about Him, and the ruling priests and Pharisees sent guards to arrest Him.

³³*Yeshua* said, "I am with you only a little while longer, and then I am going to the One who sent Me. ³⁴You will look for Me but will not find Me. Where I am, you cannot come."

³⁵The Judean leaders then said among themselves, "Where is this man about to go that we shall not find Him? He's not going to the Diaspora to teach the Greeks, is He? ³⁶What did He mean by saying, 'You will look for Me but will not find Me. Where I am, you cannot come'?"

Yeshua Satisfies Spiritual Thirsts

³⁷On the last and greatest day of the Feast, *Yeshua* stood up and cried out loudly, "If anyone is thirsty, let him come to Me and drink. ³⁸Whoever believes in Me, as the Scripture says, 'out of his innermost being will flow rivers of living water.'"ˣˣˣⁱⁱ ³⁹Now He said this about the Spirit, whom those who trusted in Him were going to receive; for the Spirit wasn't yet given, since *Yeshua* wasn't yet glorified.

⁴⁰When they heard these words, some of the crowd said, "This man really is the Prophet." ⁴¹Others were saying, "This is the Messiah." Still others were saying, "Messiah doesn't come from the Galilee, does He? ⁴²Didn't the Scripture say that the Messiah comes from the seed of David and from Bethlehem, David's town?"ˣˣˣⁱⁱⁱ ⁴³So a division arose in the crowd because of *Yeshua*. ⁴⁴Some wanted to capture Him, but no one laid hands on Him.

Religious Adversaries

⁴⁵Then the guards returned to the ruling priests and Pharisees, who asked them, "Why didn't you bring Him?"

⁴⁶"Never has anyone spoken like this man," the guards answered.

⁴⁷The Pharisees responded, "You haven't been led astray also, have you? ⁴⁸Have any of the rulers or Pharisees believed in Him? ⁴⁹No, but this mob that doesn't know the *Torah*—they are cursed!"

⁵⁰Nicodemus, the one who had come to *Yeshua* before and was one of them, said to them, ⁵¹"Our *Torah* doesn't judge a man unless it first hears from him and knows what he's doing, does it?"

⁵²They answered him, "You aren't from the Galilee, too, are you? Search, and see that no prophet comes out of the Galilee!"ˣˣˣⁱᵛ

[⁵³Then everyone went to his own house.

8 Mercy for a Sinner

¹But *Yeshua* went to the Mount of Olives. ²At dawn, He came again into the Temple. All the people were coming to Him, and He sat down and began to teach them.

³The *Torah* scholars and Pharisees bring in a woman who had been caught in adultery. After putting her in the middle, ⁴they say to *Yeshua*, "Teacher, this woman has been caught in the act of committing adultery. ⁵In the *Torah*, Moses commanded us to stone such women. So what do You say?" ⁶Now they were saying this to trap Him, so that they would have grounds to accuse Him.

But *Yeshua* knelt down and started writing in the dirt with His finger. ⁷When they kept asking Him, He stood up and said, "The sinless one among you, let him be the first to throw a stone at her." ⁸Then He knelt down again and continued writing on the ground.

⁹Now when they heard, they began to leave, one by one, the oldest ones first, until *Yeshua* was left alone with the

woman in the middle. ¹⁰Straightening up, *Yeshua* said to her, "Woman, where are they? Did no one condemn you?"

¹¹"No one, Sir," she said.

"Then neither do I condemn you," *Yeshua* said. "Go, and sin no more."]

The Light of the World

¹²*Yeshua* spoke to them again, saying, "I am the light of the world! The one who follows Me will no longer walk in darkness, but will have the light of life."

¹³Then the Pharisees said to Him, "You are testifying about Yourself, so Your testimony is not valid."

¹⁴*Yeshua* answered them, "Even if I testify about Myself, My testimony is valid. For I know where I came from and where I am going. But you don't know where I come from or where I am going. ¹⁵You judge according to the flesh, but I do not judge anyone. ¹⁶Yet even if I do judge, My judgment is true, because it is not I alone but I with the Father who sent Me.

¹⁷"Even in your *Torah* it is written that the testimony of two men is true. ˣˣˣᵛ ¹⁸I am one witness for Myself, and the Father who sent Me bears witness for Me."

¹⁹Then they said to Him, "Where is your Father?"

Yeshua answered, "You don't know either Me or My Father. If you knew Me, you would also know My Father." ²⁰He spoke these words in the treasury while teaching in the Temple, but no one arrested Him because His hour had not yet come.

Yeshua's True Origins

²¹Then again *Yeshua* spoke to them, "I am going away. You will look for Me and die in your sin. Where I am going, you cannot come."

²²"He won't kill Himself, will He?" the Judeans asked. "Is that why He says, 'Where I am going, you cannot come'?"

²³But *Yeshua* continued, "You are from below; I am from above. You are of this world; I am not of this world. ²⁴Therefore I told you that you will die in your sins. If you don't believe that I am, you will die in your sins."

Yeshua Reflects the Father's Light

²⁵So they asked Him, "Who are you?"

Yeshua replied, "Just what I'm telling you from the beginning. ²⁶I have much to say and judge about you. But the One who sent Me is true, and I tell the world what I heard from Him." ²⁷They didn't understand that He was talking to them about the Father.

²⁸So *Yeshua* said, "When you have lifted up the Son of Man, then you will know who I am. I do nothing by Myself, but speak just what the Father has taught Me. ²⁹The One who sent Me is with Me. He has not left Me alone, because I always do what is pleasing to Him."

³⁰As He was speaking these things, many people put their trust in Him.

Jewish Pedigree Is No Guarantee

³¹Then *Yeshua* said to the Judeans who had trusted Him, "If you abide in My word, then you are truly My disciples. ³²You will know the truth, and the truth will set you free!"

³³They answered Him, "We are Abraham's children and have never been slaves to anyone! How can you say, 'You will become free'?"

³⁴*Yeshua* answered them, "Amen! Amen! I tell you, everyone who sins is a slave to sin. ³⁵Now the slave does not remain in the household forever; the son abides forever. ³⁶So if the Son sets you free, you will be free indeed! ³⁷I know you are Abraham's children; yet you are trying to kill Me, because My word has no place in you. ³⁸I tell of what I have seen with the Father; so also you do what you heard from the Father."

³⁹"Abraham is our father," they replied to Him.

Yeshua said to them, "If you are Abraham's children, do the deeds of Abraham. [40]But now you are seeking to kill Me—a man who has told you the truth, which I heard from God. This Abraham did not do! [41]You are doing the deeds of your father."

They said to Him, "We were not born as illegitimate children—we have one Father, God Himself!"

[42]*Yeshua* said to them, "If God were your Father, you would love Me, for from God I came and now I'm here. For I haven't come on My own, but He sent Me. [43]Why don't you understand My speech? Because you're not able to hear My word! [44]You are of your father the devil, and you want to do the desires of your father. He was a murderer from the beginning and doesn't stand in the truth, because there's no truth in him. Whenever he speaks lies he's just being himself, because he's a liar and the father of lies.

[45]"But because I speak the truth, you do not believe Me. [46]Which one of you convicts Me of sinning? If I am telling the truth, why don't you believe Me? [47]He who belongs to God hears the words of God. The reason you don't hear[xxxvi] is because you do not belong to God."

Even Abraham Rejoiced in *Yeshua*

[48]The Judean leaders responded, "Aren't we right to say you are a Samaritan and have a demon?"

[49]*Yeshua* answered, "I do not have a demon! I honor My Father, yet you dishonor Me. [50]But I do not seek My own glory; there is One who is seeking and judging. [51]Amen! Amen! I tell you, if anyone keeps My word, he will never see death."

[52]"Now we know You have a demon!" the Judean leaders said to Him. "Abraham and the prophets died. Yet You say, 'If anyone keeps My word, he will never taste death.' [53]Surely You aren't greater than our father Abraham who died, are

You? The prophets also died! Who do You make Yourself out to be?"

[54]*Yeshua* answered, "If I glorify Myself, My glory is nothing. It is My Father who gives Me glory—the One of whom you say, 'He is our God.'[xxxvii] [55]Yet you do not know Him, but I know Him. If I say I do not know Him, I will be a liar like you. Yet I do know Him and keep His Word. [56]Your father Abraham rejoiced to see My day; he saw it and was thrilled."

[57]Then the Judeans said to Him, "You're not even fifty years old and you've seen Abraham?"[xxxviii]

[58]*Yeshua* answered, "Amen! Amen! I tell you, before Abraham came into being, I am!"

[59]Then they picked up stones to throw at Him, but *Yeshua* hid Himself and went out from the Temple.[xxxix]

9 *Yeshua* Enables the Blind to See

[1]As *Yeshua* was passing by, He saw a man who had been blind since birth. [2]His disciples asked Him, "Rabbi, who sinned, this man or his parents, that he should be born blind?"

[3]*Yeshua* answered, "Neither this man nor his parents sinned. This happened so that the works of God might be brought to light in him. [4]We must do the work of the One who sent Me, so long as it is day! Night is coming when no one can work. [5]While I am in the world, I am the light of the world."

[6]Having said these things, He spat on the ground, made mud with the saliva, and spread the mud on the blind man's eyes. [7]He told him, "Go! Wash in the Pool of Siloam" (which is translated Sent). So he went away, washed, and came back seeing.

[8]Therefore his neighbors and those who had seen him as a beggar kept say-

ing, "Isn't this the one who used to sit and beg?"

⁹"This is the one!" some said.

"No, but it looks like him," said others.

But the man himself kept saying, "I am!"

¹⁰So they asked him, "So how were your eyes opened?"

¹¹He answered, "The man who is called *Yeshua* made mud, rubbed it on my eyes, and said to me, 'Go to Siloam and wash.' So I went away and washed, and then I received my sight!"

¹²"Where is He?" they asked him.

"I don't know," he said.

Hostile Interrogation of Witnesses

¹³They bring to the Pharisees the man who once was blind. ¹⁴Now the day was *Shabbat* when *Yeshua* made the mud and opened the man's eyes. ¹⁵So again the Pharisees were asking him how he received his sight. He responded, "He put mud on my eyes, and I washed, and I see!"

¹⁶So some of the Pharisees began saying, "This man isn't from God, because He doesn't keep *Shabbat*!" But others were saying, "How can a sinner perform such signs?" So there was a split among them.

¹⁷Again they say to the blind man, "What do you say about Him, since He opened your eyes?"

And he said, "He's a prophet."

¹⁸So the Judean leaders didn't believe that he had been blind and received his sight until they called his parents. ¹⁹They questioned them, "Is this your son, whom you say was born blind? Then how does he see now?"

²⁰Then his parents answered, "We know that this is our son and that he was born blind. ²¹We don't know how he now sees, nor do we know who opened his eyes. Ask him—he's old enough. He will speak for himself." ²²His parents said

this because they were afraid of the Judean leaders. For the Judean leaders had already agreed that anyone who professed *Yeshua* to be Messiah would be thrown out of the synagogue. ²³That's why his parents said, "He's old enough—ask him."

Banning the Man Born Blind

²⁴So a second time they called the man who had been blind and said, "Give glory to God! We know that this man is a sinner!"

²⁵The man replied, "I don't know whether He's a sinner. One thing I do know is that I was blind, but now I see!"

²⁶So they asked him, "What did He do to you? How did He open your eyes?"

²⁷"I told you already and you didn't listen!" the man responded. "What, do you want to hear it again? You don't want to become His disciples too, do you?"

²⁸They railed at him and said, "You're a disciple of that man, but we're disciples of Moses! ²⁹We know that God has spoken to Moses; but as for this man, we don't know where He is from."

³⁰The man replied to them, "That's amazing! You don't know where He is from, yet He opened my eyes! ³¹We know that God doesn't listen to sinners; but if anyone fears Him and does His will, He hears this one. ³²Since the beginning of the world, no one has ever heard that anyone has opened the eyes of a man born blind. ³³If this man were not from God, He couldn't do anything."

³⁴They replied to him, "You were born completely in sin, and you're teaching us?" And they threw him out.

From Blindness to Sight

³⁵*Yeshua* heard that they had thrown him out. Finding him, He said, "Do you believe in the Son of Man?"ˣˡ

³⁶The man answered, "Who is He, Sir? Tell me, so that I may believe in Him!"

³⁷*Yeshua* said, "You have seen Him—He is the One speaking with you."

[38]He said, "Lord, I believe!" And he worshiped Him.

[39]Yeshua said, "For judgment I came into this world, so that those who don't see may see, and the ones who do see may become blind."

[40]Some of the Pharisees who were with Him heard Him say this and asked, "We're not blind too, are we?"

[41]Yeshua said to them, "If you were blind, you would have no sin. But now you say, 'We see.' So your sin remains."

10 The Faithful Hear Yeshua's Voice

[1]"Amen! Amen! I tell you, he who doesn't enter the sheepfold by the door, but climbs in some other way, is a thief and a robber. [2]But he who enters through the door is the shepherd of the sheep. [3]To him the doorkeeper opens, and the sheep hear his voice. The shepherd calls his own sheep by name and leads them out. [4]"When he has brought out all his own, he goes ahead of them; and the sheep follow him because they know his voice. [5]They will never follow a stranger, but will run away from him, for they do not know the voice of strangers." [6]Yeshua told them this parable, but they didn't understand what He was telling them.

[7]So Yeshua said again, "Amen! Amen! I tell you, I am the door for the sheep. [8]All those who came before Me are thieves and robbers, but the sheep didn't listen to them. [9]I am the door! If anyone comes in through Me, he will be saved. He will come and go and find pasture. [10]The thief comes only to steal, slaughter, and destroy. I have come that they might have life, and have it abundantly!

[11]"I am the Good Shepherd.[xli] The Good Shepherd lays down His life for the sheep. [12]The hired worker is not the shepherd, and the sheep are not his own. He sees the wolf coming and abandons the sheep and flees. Then the wolf snatches and scatters the sheep. [13]The man is only a hired hand and does not care about the sheep.

[14]"I am the Good Shepherd. I know My own and My own know Me, [15]just as the Father knows Me and I know the Father. And I lay down My life for the sheep. [16]I have other sheep that are not from this fold; those also I must lead, and they will listen to My voice. So there shall be one flock, one Shepherd.

[17]"For this reason the Father loves Me, because I lay down My life, so that I may take it up again. [18]No one takes it away from Me; but I lay it down on My own. I have the authority to lay it down, and I have the authority to take it up again. This command I received from My Father."

[19]Again a division arose among the Judeans because of these words. [20]Many of them were saying, "He has a demon. He's insane! Why listen to Him?" [21]Others said, "These are not the sayings of someone who is plagued by a demon. A demon can't open the eyes of the blind, can it?"

Despising the Light at Hanukkah

[22]Then came Hanukkah;[xlii] it was winter in Jerusalem. [23]Yeshua was walking in the Temple around Solomon's Colonnade. [24]Then the Judean leaders surrounded Him, saying, "How long will You hold us in suspense? If You are the Messiah, tell us outright!"

[25]Yeshua answered them, "I told you, but you don't believe! The works I do in My Father's name testify concerning Me. [26]But you don't believe, because you are not My sheep. [27]My sheep hear My voice. I know them, and they follow Me. [28]I give them eternal life! They will never ever perish, and no one will snatch them out of My hand. [29]My Father, who has given them to Me, is greater than all. And no one is able to snatch them out of

the Father's hand. [30]I and the Father are one."

[31]Again the Judean leaders picked up stones to stone Him. [32]*Yeshua* answered them, "I've shown you many good works from the Father. For which of these are you going to stone Me?"

[33]The Judean leaders answered, "We aren't stoning you for a good work, but for blasphemy. Though You are a man, You make Yourself God!"

[34]*Yeshua* answered them, "Isn't it written in your Writings,[xliii] 'I have said you are gods'? [35]If he called them 'gods,' to whom the Word of God came (and the Scripture cannot be broken), [36]do you say of Him, the One the Father set apart and sent into the world, 'You speak blasphemy,' because I said, 'I am *Ben-Elohim*'?

[37]"If I don't do the works of My Father, don't believe Me! [38]But if I do, even if you don't trust Me, trust the deeds. Then you may come to know and continue to understand that the Father is in Me, and I am in the Father." [39]Therefore they tried to capture Him again, but He escaped from their hand.

[40]Again He went back across the Jordan to the place where John first started immersing, and He stayed there. [41]Many people came to Him and were saying, "John performed no sign, but all John said about this man was true." [42]And many trusted in Him there.

11 Lazarus Is Dead

[1]Now a man named Lazarus was sick. He was from Bethany, the village of Miriam and her sister Martha. [2]This was the same Miriam who anointed the Master with perfume and wiped His feet with her hair. It was her brother Lazarus who was sick. [3]So the sisters sent a word to *Yeshua*, saying, "Master, the one you love is sick!"

[4]When *Yeshua* heard this, He said, "This sickness will not end in death. It is for God's glory, so that *Ben-Elohim* may be glorified through it." [5]Now *Yeshua* loved Martha and her sister and Lazarus. [6]However, when He heard that Lazarus was sick, He stayed where He was for two more days.

[7]Then after this, He said to His disciples, "Let's go up to Judea again."

[8]"Rabbi," the disciples say to Him, "just now the Judean leaders were trying to stone You! And You're going back there again?"

[9]*Yeshua* answered, "Aren't there twelve hours in the day? If a man walks in the day, he doesn't stumble, because he sees the light of the world. [10]But if a man should walk around at night, he stumbles, because the light is not in him."

[11]After He said this, He tells them, "Our friend Lazarus has fallen asleep, but I'm going there to wake him up."

[12]So the disciples said to Him, "Master, if he has fallen asleep, he will get better." [13]Now *Yeshua* had spoken about his death, but they thought He was talking about ordinary sleep.

[14]Then *Yeshua* told them clearly, "Lazarus is dead! [15]I'm glad for your sake I wasn't there, so that you may believe. Anyway, let's go to him!"

[16]Then Thomas (called Didymus[xliv]) said to the other disciples, "Let's go too, so that we may die with Him!"

Yeshua Comforts the Mourners

[17]So when *Yeshua* arrived, He discovered that Lazarus had been in the tomb already for four days. [18]Bethany was less than two miles[xlv] from Jerusalem, [19]and many of the Judeans had come to Martha and Miriam to console them about their brother.

[20]When Martha heard that *Yeshua* was coming, she went out to meet Him; but Miriam sat in the house. [21]Martha said to *Yeshua*, "Master, if You had been here, my brother wouldn't have died! [22]But I

know, even now, that whatever You may ask of God, He will give You."

²³Yeshua said to her, "Your brother will rise again."

²⁴Martha said to Him, "I know, he will rise again in the resurrection on the last day."

²⁵Yeshua said to her, "I am the resurrection and the life! Whoever believes in Me, even if he dies, shall live. ²⁶And whoever lives and believes in Me shall never die. Do you believe this?"

²⁷She says to Him, "Yes, Lord, I believe that you are the Messiah, *Ben-Elohim* who has come into the world." ²⁸After she said this, she left and secretly told her sister Miriam, "The Teacher is here, and He's calling for you." ²⁹As soon as Miriam heard, she quickly got up and was coming to Him. ³⁰Now *Yeshua* had not yet come into the village, but was still in the place where Martha had met Him. ³¹The Judeans, who were with Miriam in the house and comforting her, seeing how quickly she got up and went out, followed her. They thought she was going to the tomb to weep there.

³²So when Miriam came to where *Yeshua* was, she saw Him and fell at His feet, saying to Him, "Master, if You had been here, my brother would not have died!"

³³When *Yeshua* saw her weeping, and the Judeans who came with her weeping, He was deeply troubled in spirit and Himself agitated. ³⁴"Where have you laid him?" He asked.

"Come and see, Master," they say to Him.

³⁵*Yeshua* wept. ³⁶So the Judeans said, "See how He loved him!"

³⁷But some of them said, "Couldn't this man, who opened the eyes of the blind man, have also kept this man from dying?"

Yeshua's Word Raises the Dead

³⁸So *Yeshua*, again deeply troubled within Himself, comes to the tomb. It was a cave, and a stone was lying against it. ³⁹*Yeshua* says, "Roll away the stone!"

Martha, the dead man's sister, said to Him, "Master, by this time he stinks! He's been dead for four days!"

⁴⁰*Yeshua* says to her, "Didn't I tell you that if you believed, you would see the glory of God?"

⁴¹So they rolled away the stone. *Yeshua* lifted up His eyes and said, "Father, I thank You that you have heard Me. ⁴²I knew that You always hear Me; but because of this crowd standing around I said it, so that they may believe that You sent Me."

⁴³And when He had said this, He cried out with a loud voice, "Lazarus, come out!" ⁴⁴He who had been dead came out, wrapped in burial clothes binding his hands and feet, with a cloth over his face. *Yeshua* says to them, "Cut him loose, and let him go!"

Religious Leaders Conspire

⁴⁵Therefore many of the Judeans, who had come to Miriam and had seen what *Yeshua* had done, put their trust in Him. ⁴⁶But some of them went to the Pharisees and told them what *Yeshua* had done.

⁴⁷So the ruling priests and Pharisees called a meeting of the Sanhedrin. "What are we doing?" they asked. "This man is performing many signs! ⁴⁸If we let Him go on like this, everyone will believe in Him, and the Romans will come and take away both our holy place and our nation."

⁴⁹But one of them, Caiaphas, who was High Priest that year, said to them, "You know nothing! ⁵⁰You don't take into account that it is to your advantage that one man die for the people rather than for the whole nation to be destroyed."

⁵¹Now he did not say this by himself; but as the High Priest that year, he prophesied that *Yeshua* would die for the nation.ˣˡᵛⁱ ⁵²And not for the nation only, but also so that He might gather

together into one the scattered children of God.[xlvii]

⁵³So from that day on, they plotted to kill Him. ⁵⁴Therefore *Yeshua* no longer walked openly among the Judeans, but went from there to the country near the wilderness, to a city called Ephraim. He stayed there with His disciples.

⁵⁵Now the Jewish Passover was near; and many people went up out of the regions to Jerusalem before Passover, to purify themselves. ⁵⁶So they were searching for Yeshua, saying to one another as they stood in the Temple, "What do you think? Won't He come to the feast at all?" ⁵⁷Now the ruling priests and Pharisees had given orders that if anyone knew where He was, he should report it so that they might arrest Him.

12 Miriam Anoints the Messiah

¹Six days before Passover, *Yeshua* came to Bethany, where Lazarus was, whom *Yeshua* had raised from the dead. ²So they prepared a dinner there for *Yeshua*. Martha was serving, and Lazarus was one of those reclining at the table with Him. ³Then Miriam took a pound[xlviii] of very expensive oil of pure nard and anointed *Yeshua's* feet, and she wiped His feet dry with her hair. Now the house was filled with the fragrance of the oil.

⁴But Judah from Kriot, one of His disciples, the one who was about to betray Him, said, ⁵"Why wasn't this oil sold for three hundred denarii[xlix] and the money given to the poor?" ⁶Now he said this not because he cared about the poor, but because he was a thief. Since he had the moneybox, he used to steal from what was put in it.

⁷Therefore *Yeshua* said, "Leave her alone! She set it aside for the day of My burial. ⁸You will always have the poor among you, but you will not always have Me."

⁹Now a large crowd of Judeans knew He was there and came, not only for *Yeshua* but also to see Lazarus, whom He had raised from the dead. ¹⁰So the ruling priests made plans to kill Lazarus also, ¹¹because on account of him many of the Jewish people were going away and putting their trust in *Yeshua*.

Israel's King Has Come

¹²The next day, the huge crowd that had come up for the feast heard that *Yeshua* was coming to Jerusalem. ¹³So they took palm branches and went out to meet Him, shouting, "'*Hoshia-na*! Blessed is He who comes in the name of ADONAI!'[l] The King of Israel!"

¹⁴Finding a young donkey, *Yeshua* sat on it, as it is written, ¹⁵"Fear not, Daughter of Zion! Look! Your King is coming, sitting on a donkey's colt."[li] ¹⁶His disciples didn't understand these things at first. However, when *Yeshua* was glorified, then they remembered that these things were written about Him and that the crowd had done these things for Him.

¹⁷So the crowd, which had been with *Yeshua* when He called Lazarus out of the tomb and raised him from the dead, kept on telling everyone about it. ¹⁸It was also for this reason that the crowd came out to meet Him, because they heard that He had performed this sign. ¹⁹So the Pharisees said to each other, "You see that you can't do anything. Look, the whole world has taken off after Him!"

Fallen Seed Produces a Harvest

²⁰Now there were some Greeks among those who were going up to worship at the feast. ²¹These came to Philip, who was from Bethsaida in the Galilee. "Sir," they said, "we want to see *Yeshua*." ²²Philip comes and tells Andrew; Andrew and Philip come and tell *Yeshua*.

²³*Yeshua* answers them, saying, "The hour has come for the Son of Man to be

Miriam anoints the Messiah   John 12:1-8

"Then Miriam took a pound of very expensive oil of pure nard and anointed Yeshua's feet, and she wiped His feet dry with her hair. Now the house was filled with the fragrance of the oil." —John 12:3

glorified! [24]Amen! Amen! I tell you, unless a grain of wheat falls to the earth and dies, it remains alone. But if it dies, it produces much fruit. [25]He who loves his life will lose it, and the one who hates his life in this world will keep it forever. [26]If any man serves Me, he must follow Me; and where I am, there also will My servant be. If anyone serves Me, the Father will honor him.

[27]"Now My soul is troubled. And what shall I say? 'Father, save Me from this hour'? But it was for this reason I came to this hour. [28]Father, glorify Your name!"

Then a voice came out of heaven, "I have glorified it, and again I will glorify it!"

[29]Therefore the crowd that was standing there and heard it was saying that it had thundered. Others were saying, "An angel has spoken to Him."

[30]*Yeshua* responded, "This voice hasn't come for My sake, but for yours. [31]Now is the judgment of this world! Now the prince of this world will be driven out! [32]And as I am lifted up from the earth, I will draw all to Myself." [33]He said this to show the kind of death He was about to die.

[34]The crowd answered Him, "We've heard from *Torah* that the Messiah remains forever. How can You say, 'The Son of Man must be lifted up'? Who is this Son of Man?"

The Faithful Walk as Sons of Light

[35]Therefore *Yeshua* said to them, "The light is with you for a little longer. Walk while you have the light, so that the darkness won't overtake you. The one who walks in darkness doesn't know where he's going. [36]While you have the light, believe in the light so that you may become sons of light." *Yeshua* spoke these things, then left and hid Himself from them.

[37]But even though He had performed so many signs before them, they weren't trusting in Him. [38]This was to fulfill the word of Isaiah the prophet, who said, "Lord, who has believed our message? To whom has the arm of Adonai been revealed?"[lii]

[39]For this reason they could not believe, for Isaiah also said, [40]"He has blinded their eyes and hardened their hearts, so they might not see with their eyes nor understand with their hearts and turn back, and I would heal them."[liii] [41]Isaiah said these things because he saw His glory and spoke of Him.

[42]Nevertheless many, even among the leaders, put their trust in Him. But because of the Pharisees, they were not confessing *Yeshua*,[liv] so they wouldn't be thrown out of the synagogue;[lv] [43]for they loved the glory of men more than the glory of God.

[44]*Yeshua* cried out, "He who trusts in Me believes not in Me but in the One who sent Me! [45]And he who beholds Me beholds the One who sent Me. [46]As light I have come into the world, so that everyone who trusts in Me should not remain in darkness.

[47]"If anyone hears My words but doesn't keep them, I do not judge him; for I came to save the world, not to judge the world. [48]The one who rejects Me and doesn't receive My words has a judge; the word I spoke will judge him on the last day. [49]For I did not speak on My own, but the Father Himself who sent Me has commanded Me what to say and speak. [50]And I know that His commandment is life everlasting. Therefore, what I say, I say just as the Father has told Me."

13 Yeshua Models Purity and Humility

[1]Now it was just before the feast of Passover. *Yeshua*

knew that His hour had come to depart from this world to the Father. Having loved His own who were in the world, He loved them until the end.[lvi]

²While the *seder* meal was happening, the devil had already put in the heart of Judah from Kriot that he should hand over *Yeshua*. ³*Yeshua* knew that the Father had given all things into His hands, and that He had come from God and was returning to God. ⁴So He gets up from the meal and lays aside His outer garment; and taking a towel, He wrapped it around His waist. ⁵Then He pours water into a basin. He began to wash the disciples' feet, drying them with the towel wrapped around Him.

⁶Then He comes to Simon Peter, who says to Him, "Master, are You going to wash my feet?"

⁷*Yeshua* responded, "You don't know what I'm doing now, but you'll understand after these things."

⁸Peter said to Him, "You shall never ever wash my feet!"

Yeshua answered him, "If I don't wash you, you have no part with Me."

⁹Simon Peter said to Him, "Master, then not only my feet, but also my hands and my head!"

¹⁰*Yeshua* said to him, "He who has bathed has no need to wash, except the feet; he is completely clean. And you all are clean, though not every one." ¹¹He knew who was betraying Him; for this reason, He said, "Not all of you are clean."

¹²So after He had washed their feet and put His robe back on and reclined again, He said to them, "Do you understand what I've done for you? ¹³You call Me 'Teacher' and 'Master'; and rightly you say, for I am. ¹⁴So if I, your Master and Teacher, have washed your feet, you also ought to wash each other's feet. ¹⁵I've given you an example—you should do for each other what I have done for you.

¹⁶"Amen! Amen! I tell you, a servant isn't greater than his master, and the one who is sent isn't greater than the one who sent him. ¹⁷If you know these things, you are blessed if you do them!"

Yeshua Reveals His Betrayer

¹⁸"I'm not speaking to all of you—I know whom I have chosen. But so the Scripture may be fulfilled, 'He who eats My bread has lifted up his heel against Me.'[lvii] ¹⁹From now on I'm telling you, before it happens, so that when it happens you may believe that I am. ²⁰Amen! Amen! I tell you, he who receives the one I send, receives Me; and he who receives Me, receives the One who sent Me."

²¹After He said these things, *Yeshua* was agitated in spirit and testified, "Amen! Amen! I tell you, one of you will betray Me!"

²²The disciples began looking at each other, uncertain of whom He was speaking. ²³One of His disciples, whom *Yeshua* loved, was reclining at His side. ²⁴Simon Peter nods to him and says, "Ask Him who it is He's talking about."

²⁵Then he who leaned on *Yeshua's* chest says to Him, "Master, who is it?"

²⁶*Yeshua* answers, "It's the one I will give this bit of *matzah* to, after I dip it." After dipping the morsel, He takes it and gives it to Judah from Kriot, the son of Simon. ²⁷And with that morsel, *satan* entered into him. Then *Yeshua* tells him, "What you're about to do, do quickly!"

²⁸But no one reclining at the table knew why *Yeshua* said this to him. ²⁹Since Judah had the moneybox, some thought *Yeshua* was telling him, 'Buy what we need for the feast,' or that he should give something to the poor. ³⁰So after Judah received the bit of *matzah*, he left immediately. Now it was night.

Love Is the Grandest Legacy

³¹Then when Judah had gone out, *Yeshua* said, "Now the Son of Man is glorified, and God is glorified in Him! ³²If God is glorified in Him,[lviii] God will glorify Him in Himself, and will glorify Him at once.

³³Little children, I am with you only a little longer. You will search for Me; and just as I told the Judean leaders, so I say to you now, 'Where I am going, you cannot come.'

³⁴"I give you a new commandment, that you love one another. Just as I have loved you, so also you must love one another. ³⁵By this all will know that you are My disciples, if you have love for one another."

³⁶"Master, where are You going?" Simon Peter said to Him.

Yeshua answered, "Where I am going, you cannot follow Me now; but you will follow Me later."

³⁷Peter said to Him, "Master, why can't I follow You now? I'll lay down my life for You!"

³⁸*Yeshua* answers, "Will you lay down your life for Me? Amen! Amen! I tell you, before the rooster crows, you will deny Me three times!"

14 The Believer's Eternal Destiny

¹"Don't let your heart be troubled. Trust in God; trust also in Me. ²In My Father's house there are many dwelling places. If it were not so, would I have told you that I am going to prepare a place for you? ³And if I go and prepare a place for you, I will come again and take you to Myself, so that where I am you may also be. ⁴And you know the way to where I am going."ˡⁱˣ

⁵Thomas said to Him, "Master, we don't know where You are going. How can we know the way?"

⁶*Yeshua* said to him, "I am the way, the truth, and the life! No one comes to the Father except through Me. ⁷If you have come to know Me, you will know My Father also. From now on, you do know Him and have seen Him."

⁸Philip said to Him, "Master, show us the Father, and it is enough for us."

⁹*Yeshua* said to him, "Have I been with you for so long a time, and you haven't come to know Me, Philip? He who has seen Me has seen the Father. How can you say, 'Show us the Father'? ¹⁰Don't you believe that I am in the Father and the Father is in Me? The words I say to you, I do not speak on My own; but the Father dwelling in Me does His works. ¹¹Believe Me that I am in the Father and the Father is in Me, or at least believe because of the works themselves.

¹²"Amen! Amen! I tell you, he who puts his trust in Me, the works that I do, he will do; and greater than these he will do, because I am going to the Father. ¹³And whatever you ask in My name, that I will do, so that the Father may be glorified in the Son. ¹⁴If you ask Meˡˣ anything in My name, I will do it."

The Spirit as the Believer's Counselor

¹⁵"If you love Me, you will keep My commandments. ¹⁶And I will ask the Father, and He will give you another Helper,ˡˣⁱ so He may be with you forever. ¹⁷This is the Spirit of truth, whom the world cannot receive, because it does not behold Him or know Him. You know Him, because He abides with you and will be in you. ¹⁸I will not abandon you as orphans;ˡˣⁱⁱ I will come to you. ¹⁹In a little while, the world will no longer behold Me, but you will behold Me. Because I live, you also will live!

²⁰"In that day, you will know that I am in My Father, you are in Me, and I am in you. ²¹He who has My commandments and keeps them is the one who loves Me. He who loves Me will be loved by My Father, and I will love him and reveal Myself to him."

²²Judah (not the one from Kriot) said to Him, "Master, what has happened that You are about to reveal Yourself to us and not the world?"

²³*Yeshua* answered and said to him, "If anyone loves Me, he will keep My word. My Father will love him, and We will come to him and make Our dwelling with him. ²⁴He who does not love Me does not keep My words. And the word you hear is not Mine, but the Father's who sent Me. ²⁵These things I have spoken to you while dwelling with you. ²⁶But the Helper, the Holy Spirit, whom the Father will send in My name, will teach you everything and remind you of everything that I said to you.

²⁷*Shalom* I leave you, My *shalom* I give to you; but not as the world gives! Don't let your heart be troubled or afraid. ²⁸You've heard Me say, 'I am going away and I am coming back to you.' If you loved Me, you would rejoice that I am going to the Father, because the Father is greater than I. ²⁹I've told you now before it happens, so that when it happens you may believe!

³⁰"I won't speak with you much longer, for the ruler of this world is coming. He has nothing on Me. ³¹But in order that the world may know that I love the Father, I do exactly as the Father commanded Me.

"Get up, let's go from here!"

15 Abiding in the Life Source

¹"I am the true vine, and My Father is the gardener. ²Every branch in Me that does not bear fruit, He takes away; and every branch that bears fruit, He trims so that it may bear more fruit. ³You are already clean because of the word I have spoken to you. ⁴Abide in Me, and I will abide in you. The branch cannot itself produce fruit, unless it remains on the vine. Likewise, you cannot produce fruit unless you abide in Me. ⁵"I am the vine; you are the branches. He who remains in Me, and I in him, bears much fruit; for apart from Me, you can do nothing. ⁶If anyone does not remain in Me, he is thrown away like a branch and is dried up. Such branches are picked up and thrown into the fire and burned.

⁷"If you remain in Me and My words remain in you, ask whatever you wish, and it will be done for you. ⁸In this My Father is glorified, that you bear much fruit and so prove to be My disciples."

Residing in Love

⁹"Just as the Father has loved Me, I also have loved you. Remain in My love! ¹⁰If you keep My commandments, you will remain in My love, just as I have kept My Father's commandments and remain in His love. ¹¹These things I have spoken to you so that My joy may be in you, and your joy may be full.

¹²"This is My commandment, that you love one another, just as I have loved you. ¹³No one has greater love than this, that one lay down his life for his friends. ¹⁴You are My friends if you do what I command you.

¹⁵"I'm no longer calling you servants, for the servant doesn't know what his master is doing. Now I have called you friends, because everything I've heard from My Father I've made known to you.

¹⁶"You did not choose Me, but I chose you. I selected you so that you would go and produce fruit, and your fruit would remain. Then the Father will give you whatever you ask in My name.

¹⁷"These things I command you, so that you may love one another."

The World Hates God's Own

¹⁸"If the world hates you, know that it has hated Me before you. ¹⁹If you were of the world, the world would love you as its own. But you are not of the world, since I have chosen you out of the world; therefore, the world hates you.

²⁰"Remember the word I spoke to you, 'A servant isn't greater than his master.'[lxiii] If they persecuted Me, they

will persecute you also. If they kept My word, they will keep yours also.

²¹"But all these things they will do to you for the sake of My name, because they do not know the One who sent Me. ²²If I hadn't come and spoken to them, they would have no sin. But now they have no excuse for their sin.

²³"He who hates Me also hates My Father. ²⁴If I hadn't done works among them that no one else did, they would have no sin. But now they have seen and have hated both Me and My Father. ²⁵So is fulfilled the word written in their Scripture,ˡˣⁱᵛ 'They hated Me for no reason.'ˡˣᵛ

²⁶"When the Helper comes, whom I will send to you from the Father, the Spirit of truth who goes out from the Father, He will testify about Me. ²⁷And you also testify, because you've been with Me from the beginning."

16

¹"I have spoken these things to you so that you may be kept from stumbling. ²They will throw you out of the synagogues. Yes, an hour is coming when whoever kills you will think he is offering service to God. ³They will do these things because they have never known the Father or Me. ⁴But I have spoken these things to you so that when their hour comes, you may remember that I told you of them. I didn't tell you these things from the beginning, because I was with you."

The *Ruach* Reveals Truth

⁵"But now I am going to the One who sent Me, and not one of you is asking Me, 'Where are you going?' ⁶Because I have spoken these things to you, grief has filled your heart. ⁷But I tell you the truth, it is to your advantage that I go away! For if I do not go away, the Helper

will not come to you; but if I go, I will send Him to you.

⁸"When He comes, He will convict the world about sin, righteousness, and judgment: ⁹concerning sin, because they don't believe in Me; ¹⁰concerning righteousness, because I am going to the Father and you will no longer see Me; ¹¹and concerning judgment, because the ruler of this world has been judged.

¹²"I still have much more to tell you, but you can't handle it just now. ¹³But when the Spirit of truth comes, He will guide you into all the truth. He won't speak on His own; but whatever He hears, He will tell you. And He will declare to you the things that are to come. ¹⁴He will glorify Me, because He will take from what is Mine and declare it to you. ¹⁵Everything that the Father has is Mine. For this reason I said the Spirit will take from what is Mine and declare it to you."

Death and Resurrection Foretold

¹⁶"A little while, and you will no longer see Me. And again in a little while, you will see Me."ˡˣᵛⁱ

¹⁷Then some of His disciples said to one other, "What does He mean by telling us, 'A little while, and you will no longer see Me; and again in a little while, you will see Me'? And, 'Because I am going to the Father'?"

¹⁸They kept on saying, "What's this He's saying, 'A little while'? We don't know what He's talking about!"

¹⁹*Yeshua* knew that they wanted to question Him, so He said to them, "Are you asking each other about this, that I said, 'A little while, and you will no longer see Me; and again in a little while, you will see Me'? ²⁰Amen! Amen! I tell you, you will weep and mourn, but the world will celebrate. You will be filled with sorrow, but your sorrow will turn to joy!

²¹"When a woman is in labor she has pain, because her hour has come. But when she gives birth to the child, she no longer remembers the anguish, because

of the joy that a human being has been born into the world. ²²So also you have sorrow now; but I will see you again, and your heart will rejoice! And your joy no one will take away from you.

²³"And in that day, you will ask Me nothing. Amen! Amen! I tell you, whatever you ask the Father in My name, He will give you. ²⁴Up to now, you haven't asked for anything in My name. Ask and you will receive, so that your joy may be full.

²⁵"These things I have spoken to you in metaphors. An hour is coming when I will no longer speak to you in metaphors, but will tell you plainly about the Father. ²⁶In that day, you will ask in My name. And I'm not saying to you that I will ask the Father on your behalf. ²⁷For the Father Himself loves you, because you have loved Me and have believed that I came forth from God. ²⁸I came forth from the Father and have come into the world; again I am leaving the world and going to the Father."

²⁹His disciples say, "See, now You're speaking plainly and not in metaphors. ³⁰Now we know that You know everything and have no need to be asked anything. By this we believe that You came forth from God."

³¹Yeshua answered them, "Do you now believe? ³²Look, the hour is coming, indeed has come, when you will be scattered, each to his own. And you will leave Me alone. Yet I am not alone, because the Father is with Me. ³³These things I have spoken to you, so that in Me you may have shalom. In the world you will have trouble, but take heart! I have overcome the world!"

17 The Son Glorifies the Father

¹Yeshua spoke these things; then, lifting up His eyes to heaven, He said, "Father, the hour has come. Glorify Your Son, so the Son may glorify You. ²Even as You gave Him authority over all flesh, so may He give eternal life to all those You have given Him. ³And this is eternal life, that they may know You, the only true God, and Yeshua the Messiah, the One You sent. ⁴I glorified You on earth by finishing the work that You have given Me to do. ⁵Now, Father, glorify Me together with Yourself, with the glory which I had with You before the world came to be."

Yeshua Prays for His Talmidim

⁶"I have made Your name known to the men of this world that You gave Me. They were Yours; You gave them to Me, and they have kept Your word. ⁷Now they have come to know that everything You have given Me is from You. ⁸The words, which You gave Me, I have given to them. They received them and truly understood that I came from You, and they believed that You sent Me. ⁹I ask on their behalf. Not on behalf of the world do I ask, but on behalf of those You have given Me, for they are Yours. ¹⁰All Mine are Yours, and Yours are Mine; and I have been glorified in them. ¹¹I am no longer in the world; but they are in the world, and I am coming to You. Holy Father, keep them in Your name that You have given Me, so that they may be one just as We are. ¹²While I was with them, I was keeping them in Your name that You have given Me. I guarded them and not one of them was lost except the son of destruction,ˡˣᵛⁱⁱ so that the Scripture would be fulfilled.

¹³"But now I am coming to You. I say these words while I am still in the world, so that they may have My joy made full in themselves. ¹⁴I have given them Your word; and the world hated them, because they are not of the world just as I am not of the world. ¹⁵ I'm not asking that You take them out of the world, but that You keep them from the evil one. ¹⁶They are

not of the world, just as I am not of the world.

¹⁷"Make them holy in the truth. Your word is truth. ¹⁸Just as You sent Me into the world, so I have sent them into the world. ¹⁹And for their sakes I make Myself holy, so that they also may be made holy in truth."

Yeshua Intercedes for All Believers

²⁰"I pray not on behalf of these only, but also for those who believe in Me through their message, ²¹that they all may be one. Just as You, Father, are in Me and I am in You, so also may they be one in Us, so the world may believe that You sent Me. ²²The glory that You have given to Me I have given to them, that they may be one just as We are one—²³I in them and You In Me—that they may be perfected in unity, so that the world may know that You sent Me and loved them as You loved Me.

²⁴"Father, I also want those You have given Me to be with Me where I am, so that they may see My glory—the glory You gave Me, for You loved Me before the foundation of the world. ²⁵Righteous Father, the world didn't know You, but I knew You; and these knew that You sent Me. ²⁶I made your Name known to them, and will continue to make it known, so that the love with which You loved Me may be in them, and I in them."

18 The *Pesach* Lamb Is Arrested

¹When *Yeshua* had said these things, He went out with His disciples across the Kidron Valley,ˡˣᵛⁱⁱⁱ where there was a garden, which He and His disciples entered. ²Now Judah, who was betraying Him, also knew the place, because *Yeshua* had often met there with

His disciples. ³So Judah, having taken a band of soldiers and some officers from the ruling priests and Pharisees, comes there with lanterns, torches, and weapons.

⁴Then *Yeshua*, knowing all the things coming upon Him, went forward. He said to them, "Who are you looking for?"

⁵"*Yeshua* of *Natzeret*," they answered Him.

Yeshua tells them, "I am." And Judah, the one betraying Him, was also standing with them. ⁶So when *Yeshua* said to them, "I am," they drew back and fell to the ground.

⁷So again He asked them, "Who are you looking for?"

And they said, "*Yeshua* of *Natzeret*."

⁸*Yeshua* answered, "I told you, I am! If you're looking for Me, let these men go their way." ⁹This was so the word would be fulfilled that He spoke, "I didn't lose one of those You have given Me."ˡˣⁱˣ

¹⁰Then Simon Peter, having a sword, drew it and struck the servant of the High Priest, and cut off his right ear. Now the servant's name was Malchus. ¹¹So *Yeshua* said to Peter, "Put the sword into the sheath! The cup the Father has given Me, shall I never drink it?"

The Lamb Is Interrogated

¹²Then the band of soldiers, with the captain and the officers of the Judeans, seized *Yeshua* and tied Him up. ¹³They led Him first to Annas, for he was the father-in-law of Caiaphas, the High Priest that year. ¹⁴Now Caiaphas was the one who had advised the Judean leaders that it was advantageous for one man to die on behalf of the people.

¹⁵Simon Peter was following *Yeshua* with another disciple. Now that disciple was known to the High Priest, and he entered with *Yeshua* into the court of the High Priest. ¹⁶But Peter was left standing outside by the door. So the other disciple, who was known to the High Priest,

went out and spoke to the doorkeeper, and brought Peter in.

[17]The maidservant at the door says to Peter, "You're not one of this man's disciples also, are you?"

He says, "No, I'm not." [18]The servants and officers were standing around a fire they had made, because it was cold and they were warming themselves. And Peter was also with them, standing and warming himself.

[19]The High Priest then questioned *Yeshua* about His disciples and His teaching. [20]"I have spoken openly to the world," *Yeshua* answered him. "I always taught in the synagogues and the Temple, where all the Jews come together. I spoke nothing in secret. [21]Why question Me? Ask those who have heard what I spoke to them. Look, they know what I said."

[22]When He had said this, one of the officers standing nearby gave *Yeshua* a slap, saying, "Is that the way You answer the High Priest?"

[23]*Yeshua* answered him, "If I have spoken wrongly, give evidence of the wrong; but if rightly, why hit Me?" [24]Then Annas sent Him, still tied up, to Caiaphas the High Priest.

[25]Now Simon Peter was standing outside and warming himself. So they said to him, "You aren't one of His disciples also, are you?"

He denied it and said, "No, I'm not!"

[26]One of the servants of the High Priest, a relative of the man whose ear Peter had cut off, said, "Didn't I see you in the garden with Him?"

[27]Again Peter denied it, and immediately a rooster crowed.

The Lamb Before Politicians

[28]Then they led *Yeshua* from Caiaphas to the governor's mansion.[lxx] It was early. They themselves didn't enter the palace, so they wouldn't be made unclean, but might eat the Passover. [29]Therefore Pilate came out to them. And he said, "What charge do you bring against this man?"

[30]They answered, "If He weren't an evildoer, we wouldn't have handed Him over to you."

[31]Then Pilate said to them, "You take Him and judge Him by your *Torah!*"

The Judean leaders responded, "It is not permitted for us to put anyone to death." [32]This happened so that the word *Yeshua* spoke would be fulfilled, signifying what kind of death He was about to die.

[33]So Pilate went back into the governor's mansion, called for *Yeshua*, and asked Him, "Are you the King of the Jews?"

[34]"Are you saying this on your own," *Yeshua* answered, "or did others tell you about Me?"

[35]Pilate answered, "I'm not a Jew, am I? Your own nation and ruling priests handed You over to me! What have You done?"

[36]*Yeshua* answered, "My kingdom is not of this world. If My kingdom were of this world, then My servants would be fighting so that I wouldn't be handed over to the Judean leaders. But as it is, My kingdom is not from here."

[37]So Pilate said to Him, "Are You a king, then?"

Yeshua answered, "You say that I am a king. For this reason I was born, and for this reason I came into the world, so that I might testify to the truth. Everyone who is of the truth hears My voice."

[38]Pilate said to Him, "What is truth?" After he said this, he went out again to the Judean leaders. He said to them, "I find no case against Him. [39]But it's your custom that I release someone for you at Passover. So do you want me to release to you the King of the Jews?"

[40]They shouted back, "Not this One, but Bar-Abba!" Now Bar-Abba[lxxi] was a revolutionary.

19

The Lamb Is Bound and Sentenced

¹Then Pilate took *Yeshua* and had Him scourged. ²The soldiers twisted together a crown of thorns and put it on His head, and dressed Him in a purple robe. ³They kept coming up to Him, saying, "Hail, King of the Jews!" and slapping Him over and over.

⁴Pilate came out again. He said to them, "Look, I'm bringing Him out to you, to let you know that I find no case against Him." ⁵So *Yeshua* came out, wearing the crown of thorns and the purple robe. "Behold, the man!" Pilate said to them.

⁶When the ruling priests and officers saw Him, they yelled out, "Execute Him! Execute Him!"ˡˣˣⁱⁱ

Pilate said to them, "Take Him yourselves and execute Him! For I don't find a case against Him."

⁷The Judean leaders answered him, "We have a law,ˡˣˣⁱⁱⁱ and according to the *Torah* He must die, because He claimed to be *Ben-Elohim!*"

⁸When Pilate heard this word, he became even more fearful. ⁹He went into the governor's mansion again and said to *Yeshua*, "Where are You from?" But *Yeshua* gave him no answer. ¹⁰So Pilate said to Him, "You aren't speaking to me? Don't You know that I have the authority to release You, and I have the authority to crucify You?"

¹¹*Yeshua* answered, "You would have no authority over Me if it hadn't been given to you from above. For this reason, the one who handed Me over to you has the greater sin."

¹²Pilate tried to let Him go after this; but the Judean leaders cried out, saying, "If you release this man, you are no friend of Caesar. Everyone who makes himself a king opposes Caesar!"

¹³So when Pilate heard these words, he brought *Yeshua* out and sat down on the judge's seat at a place called the Stone Pavement, but in Aramaic,ˡˣˣⁱᵛ Gabbatha. ¹⁴It was the day of preparation for Passover, about the sixth hour.ˡˣˣᵛ And Pilate said to the Judean leaders, "Behold, your king!"

¹⁵They shouted back, "Take Him away! Take Him away! Execute Him!"

Pilate said to them, "Should I execute your king?"

The ruling priests answered, "We have no king but Caesar!"

¹⁶Finally, Pilate handed *Yeshua* over to be crucified.

The Lamb of God Is Sacrificed

¹⁷Then they took *Yeshua*. He went out, carrying His own crossbar, to the Place of a Skull, which in Aramaicˡˣˣᵛⁱ is called Golgotha. ¹⁸There they executed Him, and with Him two others, one on each side and *Yeshua* in between.

¹⁹Pilate also wrote a sign and put it on the execution stake. It was written, "YESHUA OF NATZERET, THE KING OF THE JEWS." ²⁰Many Judeans read this sign, because the place where *Yeshua* was executed was near the city; it was written in Hebrew, Latin, and Greek.

²¹The ruling priests of the Judeans were saying to Pilate, "Don't write, 'The King of the Jews,' but that He said, 'I am King of the Jews.'"

²²"What I have written, I have written," Pilate answered.

Yeshua's Surrender to Death

²³So the soldiers, when they executed *Yeshua*, took His outer garments and made four parts, a part for each soldier. They took His tunic also, but it was seamless, woven top to bottom in one piece. ²⁴So they said to one another, "Let's not tear it, but cast lots for it to see whose it will be." This was so the Scripture would be fulfilled, "They divided My garments among them, and for My clothing they

cast lots."[lxxvii] So the soldiers did these things.

²⁵Standing near the execution stake of *Yeshua* were His mother, His mother's sister, Miriam the wife of Clopas, and Miriam from Magdala. ²⁶When *Yeshua* saw His mother and the disciple whom He loved standing nearby, He said to His mother, "Woman, look at your son!" ²⁷Then to the disciple, He said, "Look at your mother!" From that very hour, the disciple took her into his own home.

²⁸After this, *Yeshua*, knowing that all things had already been completed, to fulfill the Scripture, said, "I am thirsty." ²⁹A jar full of sour wine was sitting there; so they put a sponge soaked with the sour wine on a hyssop branch and brought it to His mouth. ³⁰When *Yeshua* tasted the sour wine, He said, "It is finished!" After bowing His head, He gave up His spirit.

³¹It was the day of preparation, and the next day was a festival *Shabbat*. So that the bodies should not remain on the execution stake during *Shabbat*, the Judean leaders asked Pilate to have the legs broken and to have the bodies taken away.

³²So the soldiers came and broke the legs of the first and then the other who had been executed with *Yeshua*. ³³Now when they came to *Yeshua* and saw that He was already dead, they did not break His legs. ³⁴But one of the soldiers pierced His side with a spear, and immediately blood and water came out. ³⁵He who has seen it has testified, and his testimony is true. He knows that he is telling the truth, so that you also may believe. ³⁶These things happened so that the Scripture would be fulfilled, "Not a bone of His shall be broken."[lxxviii] ³⁷And again another Scripture says, "They shall look on Him whom they have pierced."[lxxix]

Buried in a Rich Man's Tomb

³⁸After these things, Joseph of Arimathea asked Pilate if he could take *Yeshua's* body away. Joseph was a disciple of *Yeshua*, but secretly for fear of the Judean leaders. Pilate gave permission, so Joseph came and took the body away. ³⁹Nicodemus, who had first visited *Yeshua* at night, also came, bringing a mixture of myrrh and aloes, about a hundred pounds.[lxxx] ⁴⁰Then they took the body of *Yeshua* and wrapped it in linen with the spices, as is the Jewish burial custom.

⁴¹Now in the place where He was executed, there was a garden. In the garden was a new tomb[lxxxi] where no one had yet been buried. ⁴²Because it was the Jewish day of preparation and the tomb was nearby, they laid *Yeshua* there.

20 The Lamb Is Resurrected

¹Early in the morning on the first day of the week, while it is still dark, Miriam from Magdala comes to the tomb. She sees that the stone had been rolled away from the tomb. ²So she comes running to Simon Peter and the other disciple, the one *Yeshua* loved. She tells them, "They've taken the Master out of the tomb, and we don't know where they've put Him!"

³Then Peter and the other disciple set out, going to the tomb. ⁴The two were running together, but the other disciple outran Peter and arrived at the tomb first. ⁵Bending down and looking in, he sees the linen strips lying there. But he didn't go in.

⁶Then Simon Peter comes following him. And he entered the tomb. He looks upon the linen strips lying there, ⁷and the face cloth that had been on His head. It was not lying with the linen strips, but was rolled up in a place by itself. ⁸So then the other disciple, who had reached the tomb first, also entered. He saw and believed. ⁹For they did not yet understand from Scripture that *Yeshua* must rise from the dead.[lxxxii]

"Rabboni!"   John 20:10-16

"Yeshua says to her, "Miriam!"
After she turned, she says to Him in Aramaic, "Rabboni!" (which means Teacher)." —John 20:16

Risen *Yeshua* Appears to Miriam

[10]So the disciples went away again to their own homes.

[11]But Miriam stood outside the tomb weeping. As she was weeping, she bent down to look into the tomb. [12]She sees two angels in white sitting, one at the head and one at the feet, where *Yeshua's* body had been lying.

[13]"Woman, why are you crying?" they say to her.

She says to them, "Because they took away my Master, and I don't know where they've put Him." [14]After she said these things, she turned around. And she sees *Yeshua* standing there. Yet she didn't know that it was *Yeshua*.

[15]*Yeshua* says to her, "Woman, why are you weeping? Who are you looking for?"

Thinking He's the gardener, she says to Him, "Sir, if You've carried Him away, tell me where You've put Him, and I will take Him away."

[16]*Yeshua* says to her, "Miriam!"

After she turned, she says to Him in Aramaic,[lxxxiii] "*Rabboni!*"[lxxxiv] (which means Teacher).

[17]*Yeshua* says to her, "Stop clinging to Me, for I have not yet gone up to the Father. Go to My brothers and tell them, 'I am going up to My Father and your Father, to My God and your God.'"

[18]Miriam from Magdala comes, announcing to the disciples, "I've seen the Lord," and what He had said to her.

Yeshua Extends *Shalom* to Believers

[19]It was evening on that day, the first of the week. When the doors were locked where the disciples were, for fear of the Judean leaders, *Yeshua* came and stood in their midst! And He said to them, "*Shalom aleichem!*" [20]After He said this, He showed them His hands and His side. Then the disciples rejoiced when they saw the Lord. [21]*Yeshua* said to them again,

"*Shalom aleichem!* As the Father has sent Me, I also send you."

[22]And after He said this, He breathed on them. And He said to them, "Receive the Holy Spirit! [23]If you forgive anyone's sins, they are forgiven; but if you hold back, they are held back."

The Touch of Thomas Testifies

[24]One of the twelve, Thomas called Didymus,[lxxxv] wasn't with them when *Yeshua* came. [25]The other disciples were saying to him, "We've seen the Lord!"

But he replied to them, "Unless I see the nail prints in His hands, and put my finger into the mark of the nails, and put my hand in His side, I will never believe!"

[26]Eight days later the disciples were again inside, and Thomas was with them. *Yeshua* comes, despite the locked doors. He stood in their midst and said, "*Shalom aleichem!*" [27]Then He said to Thomas, "Put your finger here, and look at My hands. Reach out your hand and put it into My side. Stop doubting and believe!"

[28]Thomas answered and said to Him, "My Lord and my God!"

[29]*Yeshua* said to Him, "Because you have seen Me, you have believed? Blessed are the ones who have not seen and yet have believed!"

[30]*Yeshua* performed many other signs in the presence of the disciples, which are not written in this book. [31]But these things have been written so that you may believe that *Yeshua* is *Mashiach Ben-Elohim*, and that by believing you may have life in His name.

21 *Yeshua* Revitalizes His *Talmidim*

[1]After these things, *Yeshua* revealed Himself again to the disciples at the Sea of Tiberias. And He manifested in this way. [2]Simon Peter,

"It's the Lord!"*   John 21:1-14

*"Therefore the disciple whom Yeshua loved says to Peter, "It's the Lord!" When Simon Peter heard that it was the Lord, he tied his outer garment around himself, for he was stripped for work, and threw himself into the sea." —John 21:7 (*see Forward)*

Thomas called Didymus, Nathanael of Cana in the Galilee, the sons of Zebedee, and two of the other disciples were together.

³Simon Peter said to them, "I'm going fishing."

"We're coming with you also," they said. They went out and got into the boat, and that night they caught nothing.

⁴At dawn, *Yeshua* stood on the beach; but the disciples didn't know that it was *Yeshua*. ⁵So *Yeshua* said to them, "Children, you don't have any fish, do you?"

"No," they answered Him.

⁶He said to them, "Throw the net off the right side of the boat, and you'll find some." So they threw the net, and they were not able to haul it in because of the great number of fish.

⁷Therefore the disciple whom *Yeshua* loved said to Peter, "It's the Lord!" When Simon Peter heard that it was the Lord, he tied his outer garment around himself, for he was stripped for work, and threw himself into the sea.

⁸But the other disciples came in the boat from about two hundred cubits^lxxxvi offshore, dragging the net full of fish. ⁹So when they got out onto the land, they saw a charcoal fire with fish placed on it, and bread.

¹⁰*Yeshua* said to them, "Bring some of the fish you've just caught."

¹¹Simon Peter went aboard and hauled the net to shore. There were 153 fish, many of them big; but the net was not broken. ¹²*Yeshua* said to them, "Come, have breakfast." None of the disciples dared ask Him, "Who are You?"—knowing it was the Lord.

¹³*Yeshua* comes and takes the bread and gives it to them, and likewise the fish. ¹⁴This was now the third time that *Yeshua* was revealed to the disciples after He was raised from the dead.

Love for *Yeshua* Rebuilds Peter

¹⁵When they had finished breakfast, *Yeshua* said to Simon Peter, "Simon son of John, do you love Me more than these?"

"Yes, Lord," he said to Him, "You know that I love you."

He said to him, "Feed My lambs!"

¹⁶He said to him again a second time, "Simon son of John,^lxxxvii do you love Me?"

"Yes, Lord," he said, "You know that I love You."

He said to him, "Take care of My sheep!"

¹⁷He said to him a third time, "Simon son of John, do you love Me?"

Peter was grieved because He said to him for a third time, "Do you love Me?" And he said to Him, "Lord, You know everything! You know that I love You!"

Yeshua said to him, "Feed My sheep!"

¹⁸"Amen! Amen! I tell you, when you were younger you used to dress yourself and walk wherever you wanted; but when you grow old you will stretch out your hands, and someone else will dress you and carry you where you do not want to go." ¹⁹Now this He said to indicate by what kind of death Peter was going to glorify God. And after this, *Yeshua* said to him, "Follow Me!"

²⁰Peter, turning around, sees the disciple following. This was the one whom *Yeshua* loved, who also had reclined against *Yeshua's* chest at the *seder* meal and said, "Master, who is the one who is betraying You?" ²¹Seeing him, Peter said to *Yeshua*, "Lord, what about him?"

²²*Yeshua* said to him, "If I want him to remain until I come, what is that to you? You follow Me!" ²³Therefore this saying went out among the brothers that this disciple would not die. Yet *Yeshua* did not say to him that he would not die, but, "If I want him to remain until I come, what is that to you?"

Epilogue

[24]This is the disciple who is testifying about these things and wrote these things. We know that his testimony is true. [25]There are also many other things that *Yeshua* did. If all of them were to be written one by one, I suppose that not even the world itself will have room for the books being written!

Tree of Life Bible

Glossary

What is the benefit to studying the glossary?

Studying the terms in the glossary will help you understand the vocabulary this Bible uses. It also introduces you to terms often used by Jewish believers in Messianic gatherings.

Where can we find the glossary words in the text?

At the end of every definition in this glossary you will find a chapter and verse reference in **boldface**. This will show you a place where that word is used in context. Looking up those Scriptures can be a good way to learn the meanings of these words.

Why are some words italicized?

In this translation, the italicized words (such as *Elohim*) are transliterated Hebrew. This means we use English letters to represent Hebrew sounds. The transliteration allows you to become familiar with the sounds of spoken Hebrew and may encourage you to learn written Hebrew as well.

How do I say the Hebrew transliterated words?

Unlike in English, each vowel sound in Hebrew nearly always has the same sound. Use this chart to help with the pronunciation of the vowels:

"a" sounds like the a in father

"e" sounds like the e in sent

"i" sounds like the i in sphagetti

"ei" sounds like the ey in they

"ai" sounds like the ai in aisle

"u" sounds like the u in truth

"o" sounds like the o in go

"y" sounds like the y in yes

an ' sounds like a very short a, as in about

The consonants are easier. Most of them are like English with a few exceptions:

"h" as in holy

"tz" as in the zz in pizza

"ch" as in Bach

Lastly, on what syllable do you put the emphasis in Hebrew? Hebrew words often have their accent on the second half of the word, the opposite of English. But there are many exceptions. So in this glossary we will put the syllable to be accented in bold. And while actual Hebrew writing is read from right to left, when reading the transliteration, read from left to right as in English.

ADONAI —Hebrew for "LORD." When it is in small capitals (LIKE THIS), it refers to God's personal name as given in the Hebrew Bible, which is YHWH. This personal name is God's "covenant name," used when God is relating to the Jewish people in an intimate way. Since its pronunciation is not known, and also out of respect for God's name, Jews traditionally substitute the word ADONAI. Compare the entry for Elohim (John 1:23).

Amen —At the end of a sentence, this word means, "Let it be so" indicating that the readers or listeners agree with what was just said. At the start of a phrase, it means, "This is a truth you can believe in and live by" (John 10:1).

angel—A supernatural messenger sent by God (John 20:12).

anointed—Set apart by God for a task. In the Tanakh, kings and priests were anointed by the application of oil. The word "Messiah" means "Anointed One." In this case it doesn't mean that the Messiah had oil put on him, but that God set him apart for the task of being the Redeemer. See also the entries for Mashiach and Messiah (John 1:41).

Ben-Elohim —One of Yeshua's titles, meaning "Son of God" (John 11:4).

blasphemy—Profaning God's name by cursing Him or speaking slander against Him or His Word (John 10:33).

circumcision—The removal of the foreskin of males on the eighth day after birth. Circumcision is the sign of the covenant God made with the Jewish people. In Hebrew, it is called brit milah (John 7:22).

commandment—An order given by God to His people, or by Yeshua. There are 613 commandments in the Torah. The Hebrew term is mitzvah (plural, mitzvot) (John 13:34).

demon—An evil spirit who is an agent of satan (John 8:49).

diaspora—The dispersion or scattering of the Jewish people throughout the world. The term is actually Greek; the corresponding Hebrew term is galut meaning "exile" (John 7:35).

disciple—A student and follower of a teacher, who not only learns the teacher's wisdom, but even more importantly, also models his life on that of the teacher. In Hebrew, a disciple is called a talmid, and the plural is talmidim (John 1:35).

Elohim —"God" in general terms, or as Creator. Compare the entry for ADONAI, God's "covenant name," used especially in His relationship to the Jewish people. Elohim is the plural form of El , also found in the Bible occasionally with the same meaning.

Father—God, the King of the universe, in His relation to Yeshua (John 5:18).

fulfill—Accomplish, carry out, or fill full with meaning. The word is found in relation to Scripture or to the words of *Yeshua*, showing that something previously spoken about has now happened **(John 19:36).**

Galileans—See entry for Judeans.

Gentiles, nations—The term for individuals or people groups who are not Jewish. In Hebrew a common word for Gentiles is *goyim.*

glory—The manifestation of God's presence and power, especially in a visible way **(John 2:11).**

grace—Undeserved favor that God gives to His people **(John 1:16).**

Greek—The language spoken in Greece; also a term for people who spoke Greek, or participate in the Greek culture.

Hanukkah —A holiday whose name means "dedication." The Feast of Dedication commemorates the victory of the Maccabees over the armies of Antiochus Epiphanes in 165 B.C.E. and the rededication of the Temple after it had been defiled **(John 10:22).**

holy—Set apart for God's purposes. God Himself radiates holiness. In Hebrew, the term is *kadosh* **(John 17:11).**

hoshia-na —"Hosanna" in English, a term meaning, "Save us please," which is found in the *Tanakh* in Psalm 118:25 **(John 12:13).**

immerse—To ceremonially dip the whole body under water as an act of dedication to the Lord or as a profession of faith in *Yeshua.* The word is often seen in other translations as "baptize." The act of dipping is called "immersion" or, in other translations, "baptism." The Hebrew term is *tevilah* **(John 1:26).**

intercede—To pray on behalf of another person. The person who prays is called an "intercessor" or a "mediator," which is someone who comes between God and people in order to help them **(John 17:20, Heading).**

Israel—The name given by God to His chosen people, the Jews. The term refers to the people as a whole, and also to the land where the ten northern tribes lived. In modern times, it refers to the nation established in 1948 as the Jewish homeland **(John 1:49).**

Jerusalem—The royal city from which the kings of Israel ruled and the place where the Holy Temple was located. Sometimes called "the city of peace," it also refers to the heavenly Jerusalem of the future. Its name in Hebrew is *Yerushalayim* **(John 2:13).**

Jews, Jewish—The Jews are God's chosen people, descended from Abraham, Isaac, and Jacob, with whom He made His covenants. God gave the Torah to the Jewish people and promised them the land of Israel. "Jewish" is the word that describes this people or anything that has to do with them, such as holidays and ceremonies **(John 19:19, John 2:13).**

Judeans—The people living in Judea, which was the southern part of Israel. In earlier Jewish history, it was known as the Kingdom of Judah. Judean leaders in Jerusalem tended to look down on the people who lived in Galilee, called "Galileans," because the Judeans thought they were less sophisticated **(John 5:16)**.

kingdom of God—The reality of God's rulership in our lives now and throughout all the world in the age to come **(John 3:3)**.

Lord—A term of respect given to *Yeshua*, recognizing His divine identity. See also the entries for Master, ADONAI **(John 21:7)**.

manna —The bread from heaven that God gave to our people in Exodus 16 as they wandered the desert after being redeemed from slavery in Egypt **(John 6:31)**.

Mashiach —The Anointed One, called in English the Messiah, who was foretold by the Hebrew Scriptures. In Greek, the word is *Christos*, from which we get the English term "Christ." See also the entry for anointed **(John 20:31)**.

Master—A term of respect, recognizing a teacher's authority **(John 13:14)**.

matzah —Unleavened bread, which is made without yeast, eaten especially during the feast of Passover **(John 13:26)**.

Messiah—See entry for *Mashiach* **(John 1:41)**.

nations—See entry for Gentiles.

Natzeret —Nazareth, the town in south central Galilee where *Yeshua* grew up. The name comes from the Hebrew word *netzer*, which means "branch." A clan from the line of David founded this town **(John 19:19)**.

pagans—A term used for worshippers of foreign gods or idols. It does not have the same meaning as "Gentiles," which refers to any non-Jews, including followers of Yeshua.

Passover—The Jewish festival during which Jews used to journey to the Temple, sacrifice lambs, and eat a special meal commemorating the departure of the Jews from slavery in Egypt. Today it is celebrated with a service in the home called the *seder*. The holiday in Hebrew is called *Pesach*. See also the entry for *seder* **(John 13:1, John 18:1, Heading)**.

Pharisees—One of the sects of Judaism in the first century. The Pharisees had their own views of how exactly to keep *Torah*. They were especially concerned with ritual purity and (unlike the Sadducees) they believed in the resurrection of the dead. While the Sadducees were more involved with the Temple, the Pharisees were concerned more with home and synagogue life. The Hebrew term is *P'rushim* **(John 4:1)**.

priests—Men who offered sacrifices and performed other religious rituals at the Temple in Jerusalem. They were descended from Aaron, the brother of Moses. The Hebrew term is *kohanim* . The priests were mostly from the Sadducee sect of Judaism. See the entry for Sadducees **(John 11:47)**.

rabbi—A highly esteemed teacher who trained disciples. The title comes from a Hebrew word meaning "my great one" **(John 4:31)**.

Rabboni —A title meaning "my teacher." It is a variant of "rabbi" **(John 20:16)**.

resurrection—The act of rising from the dead back to life. Also used to refer to the time at the end of history when God will raise the dead **(John 11:25)**.

righteous—Morally good, virtuous **(John 17:25)**.

ritual—An established procedure for performing religious acts **(John 2:6)**.

Romans—The people who ruled over the entire Mediterranean world, including Israel, during the time of *Yeshua* (as well as before and after). Their territory was called the "Roman Empire" **(John 11:48)**.

Sadducees—One of the sects of Judaism in the first century. From the Sadducees came most of the priests who officiated in the Temple. In contrast to the Pharisees, they did not believe in the resurrection of the dead. See also the entry for priests and for Pharisees.

salvation—God's saving acts in human history. For Israel, salvation means deliverance from enemies or exile as well as national deliverance from God's judgment, leading to peace and long life in the homeland. Salvation, with respect to individuals, also refers to deliverance from God's judgment. For *Yeshua's* faithful followers, salvation begins in this life and leads to everlasting life in God's presence in the age to come **(John 4:22)**.

Samaritans—A people descended from a mix of Israelites and other nations that the Assyrians brought to Samaria, as told in 2 Kings 17. The Samaritans practiced an offshoot of Judaism and thought that the Temple in Jerusalem was not a legitimate place to worship. Jewish people and Samaritans did not think well of one another **(John 4:8)**.

Sanhedrin—The highest council of the Jews, exercising legislative and judicial authority **(John 11:47)**.

satan —The chief fallen angel who opposes God's will on earth. He is the accuser of humanity who tries to undermine God's people and God Himself. *Satan* is a Hebrew word that means "adversary" **(John 13:27)**.

Savior—A title of *Yeshua*, in recognition of His work in making salvation from sin and its consequences possible for all people both Jewish and Gentile. See also the entry for salvation **(John 4:42)**.

Scripture—The Hebrew Bible, known in Hebrew as the *Tanakh*. Christians commonly call it the "Old Testament." Today we use the term "Scripture" to include the New Covenant as well, which was not yet written down in the days of *Yeshua* **(John 19:36)**.

seder —Literally "order," this term refers to the ceremonial meal commemorating Passover. See also the entry for Passover **(John 13:2)**.

Shabbat —The Sabbath, the seventh day of the week. On this day we are to rest and renew our relationship with our Creator, who also rested on the seventh day. *Shabbat* begins on Friday evening at sundown and ends at sundown on Saturday **(John 9:14)**.

shalom —The Hebrew word for "peace." It is also used as a greeting ("hello"), as a farewell ("goodbye"), and also signifies wholeness and well-being **(John 14:27)**.

shalom aleichem —A greeting that means "peace be with you" **(John 20:19)**.

sinner—a person who violates the commandments of God **(John 9:24)**.

Son of Man—A name that Yeshua commonly uses to refer to Himself. It comes from Daniel 7:13-14, in which the "Son of Man" is given all authority. This name sometimes emphasizes Yeshua's humanity and sometimes His deity **(John 6:27)**.

Spirit—The Spirit of God is the One who inspires the prophets, anoints the Messiah, and empowers His followers. The Hebrew term is *Ruach* **(John 7:39)**.

Sukkot —The Feast of Booths or Tabernacles. This holiday came in the fall at the time of the grape harvest and was a time of great rejoicing. The Hebrew word *sukkah* means "booth." *Sukkot* is the plural and can mean either "booths" or the name of this holiday. See also the entry for Tabernacle, tabernacle **(John 7:1, Heading)**.

synagogue—A place of assembly of Jews for hearing the *Torah*, praying, and worshipping God. There were many synagogues throughout Israel **(John 9:22)**.

Tabernacle, tabernacle—A temporary dwelling. It is used of the booths constructed during the Feast of Tabernacles. It is also used in the *Tanakh* of the tent in which God dwelt among the Jewish people in the wilderness and in the land of Israel. When tabernacle is used as a verb, it refers to *Yeshua* coming to dwell among His people, reminding us of the wilderness Tabernacle and also the Feast of Tabernacles **(John 7:2, John 1:14)**.

talmid, talmidim —See entry for disciple.

Tanakh—The Hebrew Scriptures. Tanakh is a word made up of the first letters of Torah, Nevi'im (Prophets), and Ketuvim (Writings). A word made up of the first letters of other words is called an "acronym." So T + N + K becomes Tanakh.

Temple—The magnificent building in Jerusalem designated by God for sacrifices and worship. It was destroyed in the year 70 CE by the Roman armies **(John 2:14)**.

testimony—Evidence given by a witness, who is someone who sees and reports something **(John 1:19 ("testimony"), 1:7 ("witness"))**.

Torah (also commonly pronounced *Torah*) —Literally "instruction," this term can refer to the five books of Moses or more generally to God's commandments. Some Jews distinguish the Written Torah from the Oral Torah, which was transmitted by oral tradition until being written down at the end of the second century CE. See also the entry for commandment **(John 7:19)**.

witness—See entry for testimony.

works—Actions one does in order to obey God and His Word **(John 6:28)**.

worship—Reverent honor paid to God **(John 4:22)**.

Yeshua —The Hebrew name of our Messiah, known in English as "Jesus." The name means "salvation" **(John 19:19)**.

Zion—A mountain in Jerusalem (Mount Zion). The name is more generally used to refer to Jerusalem as a whole or to the land of Israel. In Hebrew, it is called *Tziyon* **(John 12:15)**.

Endnotes

i............1:1. cf. Gen. 1:1; Prov. 8:23.

ii...........1:14. cf. Exod. 40:34.

iii..........1:18. Some mss. say *the only Son.*

iv..........1:23. Is. 40:3.

v...........1:29. cf. Exod. 12:21; Num. 28:8; Is. 53:5-7.

vi..........1:49. cf. Ps. 2:6-7.

vii.........1:51. cf. Gen. 28:12-13; Dan. 7:13.

viii........2:6. About 20-25 gallons; 1 measure is about 9 gallons.

ix..........2:12. Some mss. say *brothers and sisters.*

x...........2:17. Ps. 69:10(9).

xi..........3:3, 7. Or *born again*

xii.........3:5. cf. Ezek. 36:24-27.

xiii........3:14. cf. Num. 21:8.

xiv........3:19. cf. Is. 5:20.

xv.........4:5. Near Shechem, cf. Gen. 33:19.

xvi........4:6. Lit. *about the sixth hour.*

xvii.......4:25. *Christ* (Gk.) and *Messiah* (Heb.) both mean *Anointed One.*

xviii......4:52. One o'clock.

xix........5:2. Lit, *in Hebrew.* Bethesda (Heb.) means *House of Mercy.* Bethzatha (Aram.) means *the place of poured out water.*

xx .... 5:3. ASV adds: *They waited for the water to be moved.* Other mss. also add verse 4: *because an angel of the Lord sometimes went to the pool and moved the water. Then, whoever went into the water first was healed from whatever disease he had.*

xxi ....5:28-29. cf. Ezek. 37:12; Ps. 16:10; Dan. 12:2.

xxii........5:46-47. cf. Deut. 18:15-19.

xxiii.......6:7. One denarius was the daily wage for a laborer.

xxiv.......6:14. cf. Dt. 18:15.

xxv ....6:19. About three or four miles, halfway across the sea.

xxvi ......6:20. Lit. *I am. Don't be afraid;* cf Jn. 8:24, 18:6.

xxvii......6:31. Ps. 78:24; cf. Exod. 16:4-36; Neh. 9:15.

xxviii.....6:41. Perhaps *Galileans.*

xxix ......6:45. cf. Isa 54:13.

xxx ....7:2. cf. Deut. 16:16.

xxxi ......7:15. Lit. *knows letters, not having learned.*

xxxii .....7:38. cf. Is. 44:3, 55:1, 58:11; Ezek. 47; Zech. 14:8.

xxxiii.....7:42. cf. Mic. 5:1(2).

xxxiv ....7:52. The earliest manuscripts do not include John 7:53-8:11.

xxxv .....8:17. cf. Dt. 17:6; 19:15.

xxxvi ....8:47. Dt. 6:4; Ex. 24:7.

xxxvii ...8:54. Some mss. say *your God.*

xxxviii ..8:57. Some mss. say *has Abraham seen You?*

xxxix ....8:59. Some mss. add *passing through their midst, he went away in this manner.*

xl..........9:35. Some mss. say *the Son of God (Ben-Elohim).*

xli.........10:11. cf. Gen. 48:15; Ps. 23; Ezek. 37:24.

xlii........10:22. Lit. *Rededication.*

xliii....... 10:34. Lit. *Law,* here applied to Torah, Prophets, and Writings; quote is from Ps. 82:6.

xliv........11:16. "the Twin."

xlv.........11:18. Lit. 15 stadia; 1 stadion is about 607 feet or 187 meters.

xlvi........11:51. cf. Is. 53:8.

xlvii.......11:52. cf. Is. 11:10-11; 56:6-7; Jer. 3:17; Mic. 2:12-13.

xlviii......12:3. A Roman pound, about 12 ounces.

xlix........12:5. One denarius was the daily wage for a laborer.

l............12:13. Ps. 118:25-26.

li...........12:15. Zech. 9:9.

lii..........12:38. Is. 53:1.

liii.........12:40. cf. Is. 6:10.

liv..........12:42. cf. Jn. 9:22.

lv...........12:42. Lit. *from the synagogue*, i.e., excommunicated, cut off from all community, banned; cf. Mt. 18:17.

lvi..........13:1. cf. John 19:30.

lvii.........13:18. cf. Ps. 41:10(9).

lviii........13:32. Early mss. missing this first part.

lix..........14:4. Some mss. say *Where I am going you know, and the way you know.*

lx...........14:14. Some mss. omit *Me.*

lxi..........14:16. *Intercessor, Advocate, Comforter,* or *Counselor*; lit. *Paraclete.* Also in 14:26;
15:26; 16:7.

lxii.........14:18. cf. Exod. 22:21-23(22-24); Jer. 49:11.

lxiii........15:20. Jn. 13:16.

lxiv........15:25. Lit. *Torah* or *the Law*; cf. Lk. 24:44-45.

lxv.........15:25. cf. Ps. 35:19; 69:5(4); *sinat chinam.*

lxvi........16:16. Some mss.add "because I go to the Father."

lxvii.......17:12. cf. Ps. 41:10(9).

lxviii......18:1. cf. 2 Sam. 15:23.

lxix........18:9. Similar to Jn. 6:39, 17:12.

lxx ....18:28, 33; 19:9. Lit. *Praetorium.*

lxxi........18:40. *Son of Abba* or *Son of the Father* (Aram.).

lxxii.......19:6. Lit. *crucify* or *crucified* in 19:6, 10, 15, 16, 18, 20, 23, 32, 41; a Roman method
of execution.

lxxiii......19:7. cf. Lev. 24:16

lxxiv......19:13. Lit. *in Hebrew.*

lxxv ......19:14. i.e., noon.

lxxvi .....19:17. Lit. *in Hebrew.*

lxxvii.....19:24. Ps. 22:19(18).

lxxviii....19:36. cf. Ex. 12:46; Num. 9:12; Ps. 34:21(20).

lxxix .....19:37. Zech. 12:10.

lxxx ......19:39. Roman pound = 12 ounces; 100 Roman pounds = 75 pounds.

lxxxi .....19:41. cf. Is. 53:9.

lxxxii ....20:9. cf. Ps. 16:10.

lxxxiii....20:16. Lit. *in Hebrew.*

lxxxiv ...20:16. Aramaic for *my rabbi* or *my great one.*

lxxxv ....20:24. Lit. *the Twin.*

lxxxvi ...21:8. One cubit is about 18 inches.

lxxxvii ..21: 16 & 17. Some mms. "Simon son of Jonah"

www.TreeOfLifeBible.org

If you would like to contribute financially to the development of this newly vetted, theologically sound text, you are welcome to learn more about our project and donate online. Rest assured that this text is owned by our not-for-profit corporation and no one will ever be allowed to alter this Biblical text without our written approval.

The ongoing purpose of our corporation is to create and subsidize the distribution of a new Messianic Jewish Version of the Holy Bible to all mankind. All contributions brought in that exceed our need to meet the expenses to complete this new text will go directly to purchasing more bibles to distribute freely to everyone who wants to learn of our Messiah.

Our declaration is that *Yeshua*, Jesus, laid down His life willingly as our eternal offering for sin. We further acknowledge we believe He rose from the dead three days later and sits now at the right hand of God in heaven. We want the whole world to know He is the Son of God.

www.DestinyImage.com

Destiny Image Publishing is our exclusive publisher of this new version and has committed to partnering with us for the duration of this project. When you want to purchase more copies of this book, and the others to follow, go to their website. Help us get this bible into the hands of everyone you know that needs Messiah! And, be sure to tell your entire social network about us on Facebook and Twitter, too!

The active role of Destiny Image in furthering this project, both financially and professionally, is a blessing for Messianic Jewish believers worldwide. Their commitment to stand with us, to pray for us, to encourage us and to work alongside us is a living example of the brotherly love that changes the world. That is the message of hope and acceptance that *Yeshua's* message is still about!

Behold how good and how pleasant it is for brother's to dwell together in unity. May God's grace and mercy overflow Donald Nori and the entire Destiny Image family, forever in Yeshua's love.

God bless and keep you,

Daniah Greenberg, President
Messianic Jewish Family Bible Project
spreadtheword@messianicfamilybible.org

DESTINY IMAGE PUBLISHERS, INC.

*"Speaking to the Purposes of God for This Generation
and for the Generations to Come."*

VISIT OUR NEW SITE HOME AT
WWW.DESTINYIMAGE.COM

FREE SUBSCRIPTION TO DI NEWSLETTER

Receive free unpublished articles by top DI authors, exclusive

discounts, and free downloads from our best and newest books.

Visit www.destinyimage.com to subscribe.

Write to: Destiny Image

           P.O. Box 310

           Shippensburg, PA 17257-0310

Call: 1-800-722-6774

Email: orders@destinyimage.com

For a complete list of our titles or to place an order
online, visit www.destinyimage.com.

FIND US ON FACEBOOK OR FOLLOW US ON TWITTER.

www.facebook.com/destinyimage   **facebook**
www.twitter.com/destinyimage   **twitter**